Correct Mispronunciations of Some South Carolina Names

By Claude and Irene Neuffer

The Indian Maiden (probably Fictional)
who rode from Pickens To Ninety-Six SC.
Was named Caleechee (and also called
Isaqueena. See p. 31 and p. 89.

UNIVERSITY
OF
SOUTH CAROLINA PRESS

MUNGO = WAS AN ANCESTOR OF FRANK DRC
(Great Grandmother?) named MUNGO? (April 2000)

Copyright © University of South Carolina 1983
Published in Columbia, South Carolina, by the
University of South Carolina Press

First Printing, 1983
Second Printing, 1983
Third Printing, 1984
Fourth Printing, 1987
Fifth Printing, 1991
Manufactured in the United States of America

Library of Congress Cataloging in Publication Data
Neuffer, Claude Henry.
    Correct mispronunciations of some South Carolina
names.

    1. Names, Geographical—South Carolina. 2. Names,
Personal—South Carolina—Pronunciation. 3. English
language—South Carolina—Pronunciation. 4. South
Carolina—History, Local. I. Neuffer, Irene.
II. Title.
F267.N39   1983   917.57'0014   83–5947
ISBN 0–87249–424–1

ISBN 0-87249-556-6 (pbk)

Pronunciation Key

We have spelled each name phonetically without using the diacritical marks of the International Phonetic Alphabet found in most dictionaries. The key below provides our spellings of various sounds in the left column and common words in which the sounds occur in the right column. If the reader is in doubt about the sound represented by the last syllable in the phonetic spelling YOO-JEE (Huger), for instance, he may consult the key for assistance. There he will find that "J" is pronounced as in "just" and "EE" as in "heat"; so the final syllable of this name sounds like our exclamation, "Gee." Two general principles: long vowels are all represented with a final "e" whether or not there is an intermediary consonant ("pie," "kite," "toe" and "hope" are all words with long vowels in which our phonetic spellings would agree exactly with the conventional spellings); vowels followed by the "r" sound are all spelled phonetically as a vowel plus "h" ("huhr" for "her")— even when we don't pronounce the "r" as our Northern neighbors and the dictionaries insist we should. Accented syllables are capitalized; unaccented syllables are in small letters—e.g., Edisto is spelled phonetically ED-is-TOE. No distinction has been made among accented syllables receiving slightly different degrees of stress.

a	cat	ow	now; out
ah	father; car	s	since
aw	awful; ought	sh	sugar; shape
ae/a + final e	ate; pain	th	thin
ch	chat	*th*	that
e	beg	u	but
ee	heat	ue/ u + final e	mule
eeh	pier; fear	uh	agree; happen;
eh	there; care		terrible; mo-
g	get		lasses; stirrup
i	hit		(this is the un-
ie/ i + final e	pie; kite		accented little
j	just; gin		grunt some-
k	kit; car;		times called a
	character		schwa)
ng	thing	UH	urge; her
o	hot	wh	which
oe/ o + final e	toe; hope	y	yet
oh	for	z	cards; zero
oi	noise; boy	zh	leisure

Preface

Among Americans, South Carolinians have done more than any other group to carry on the fine old English tradition of pronouncing a name one way and spelling it another. The classic English examples are Cholmondeley, which is pronounced CHUM-lee, and Pontrefact, which is pronounced POM-fret. The classic South Carolina example is Huger, which is pronounced YOO-JEE, to the consternation of long-distance truck drivers from other states who sometimes suppose that a stranger is greeting their arrival with an exclamation of surprise (*You! Gee!*).

Of course, there is probably no word in the English language that isn't pronounced in different ways by different people, even if the differences are sometimes too subtle to be perceived by anyone other than a trained phoneticist. Which pronunciation is the "correct" one? For the purposes of this little book we take the correct pronunciation of a family name to be the one the family uses, and the correct pronunciation of a place name to be the one that has traditionally been preferred by most reasonably well-educated people in the neighborhood.

By "correct mispronunciations" we mean, of course, pronunciations that are considered correct in South Carolina but will seem wrong to you if you've just arrived from Connecticut, bless your sun-seeking heart, and you've never been in the Palmetto State before.

We'd like to preserve these traditional pronunciations. We are South Carolinians and to a South Carolinian the impulse to preserve a tradition is almost as instinctive as breathing. Where else but in South Carolina would you find names like States Rights Gist or Mary John C. Calhoun Happoldt?

A lot of the names that give people trouble are those that French Huguenots, fleeing persecution, brought with them to South Carolina. Sometimes you pronounce them more or less the way a modern Frenchman would, but some names have preserved a French spelling and peculiarly South Carolinian pronunciation. For instance Legaré is pronounced *luh-GREE*.

When Harriet Beecher Stowe, in *Uncle Tom's Cabin*, assigned the name Simon Legree to one of the most unpleasant characters in American fiction, she didn't invent the name Legree. She had heard the South Carolina name. Perhaps she changed the spelling because she didn't expect her readers to be able to cope with the spelling Legaré. Perhaps she simply didn't know the correct spelling (there was a great deal she didn't know about the South). The most charitable explanation may be that she knew there were many charming, sensitive, intelligent, and strikingly unvillainous people called Legaré in South Carolina and wished to spare them embarrassment even though she found the *sound* of the name irresistible.

German, Spanish, and African ways of speaking have also influenced the pronunciations (and occasionally the spellings) of South Carolina names, as have the languages of various Indian groups.

Then there's the story about the three dogs who met at the corner of Broad Street and Meeting Street in Charleston. One of them was a mongrel who said, "I'm from New York and my name is Spot. That's spelled S-P-O-T." Another was a German Shepherd who said, "I'm from Ohio and my name is Rover. That's spelled R-O-V-E-R." The third was a French Poodle who said,

"Welcome to Charleston. My name is Fido and that's spelled P-H-I-D-E-A-U-X."

In no way can we claim that this little lexicon is definitive. In some cases we have discussed the origin of a name for no better reason than that it pleased us to do so, and the reader should bear in mind that, as A. L. Pickens has warned us, there are very few Indian words of whose meaning we can be completely sure "unless we are blessed with the happy certainty of the uninformed."

There are a few names in this book whose pronunciations really are not problematic but which we dragged in by the scruffs of their delightful necks because we simply couldn't resist the opportunity to say a word or two about them. It was a Yankee, Ralph Waldo Emerson, who declared that "A foolish consistency is the hobgoblin of little minds," and we are large-mindedly content to enjoy his license to ramble a little, without making a great effort to be punctiliously systematic. We hope, nevertheless, that this opinionated dictionary of too-frequently mispronounced names will be helpful to broadcasters and to newcomers who'd like to pronounce the names of local people and places in the ways that South Carolinians have traditionally preferred. And we hope that longtime South Carolinians will find some interesting morsels of history that they hadn't known before.

In compiling this book, we have drawn heavily on our experience of editing *Names in South Carolina* for twenty-nine years. By their contributions to that annual publication the following have helped to make this book possible:

Caroline Picault Aimar, Susan Lowndes Allston, Lynda S. Alsup, Thomas Ancrum, Ed L. Anderson, Sallie B. Anderson, Robert L. Ariail, Elizabeth Atkinson, Havilah Babcock, Robert Duncan Bass, Wade T. Batson, Robert P. Bell, John Townsend Benton, Connelly Burgin Berry, Albert D. Betts, John A. Bigham, Eugene H. Blake, U. Hoyt Bodie, Caroline Bokinsky, Rendy L. Boland, Herman Wye Boozer, Hope Boykin, Francis W. Bradley, Marguerite Brennecke, Edwin M. Brogdon, Louis C. Bryan, Gertrude C. Bull, Elias B. Bull, David F. Bullard, Ronald D. Burnside, Mark W. Buyck, Jr., Cordelia Bearden Campbell, J. M. Campbell, Buford S. Chappell, Eugene B. Chase, Jr., Thelma Chiles Clark,

Kenneth D. Coates, R. W. Coggeshall, J. Rutledge Connor, Frank
Covington, E. T. Crowson, William P. Cumming, Rosalee M. Cur-
tis, Chalmers Gaston Davidson, Ted M. Davis, Edith Bannister
Dowling, Mary J. Drayton, Alderman Duncan, Jean Eastman,
J. H. Eleazer, Christie Z. Fant, Marcus Field, Mabel Trott Fitz-
simons, Viola Gaston Floyd, John Foxworth, Edna R. Foy, Evelyn
McD. Frazier, W. E. Fripp, Lee R. Gandee, Thomas J. Gasque,
Paul M. Gettys, Lloyd G. Gibbs, Anne C. Gibert, Emily Smith
Glenn, W. Marvin Graveley, James H. Hammond, Harry R. E.
Hampton, John T. Harllee, William L. Harrelson, Joseph E. Hart,
Jr., Dan Manville Hartley, James L. Haynsworth, P. F. Hender-
son, Cornelia H. Hensley, Marion M. Hewell, A. C. (Zan) Hey-
ward, Theresa M. Hicks, Daniel W. Hollis, J. Oscar Hunter, John
L. Idol, Jr., Nexsen Johnson, Frel M. Johnstone, Katherine M.
Jones, William S. Kable, James E. Kibler, James C. Kinard, Fran-
cis Marion Kirk, Kenneth K. Krakow, Pierre F. LaBorde, Alberta
Morel Lachicotte, Edward B. Latimer, Thomas O. Lawton, Jr.,
Xania F. Lawton, J. M. Lesesne, Terry M. Lipscomb, Gideon M.
Long, Robert L. Mackintosh, Jr., Carroll Davis Martin, Vanetha
S. Matthews, Carl. H. May, Nellie Chappell Maybin, Drayton
Mayrant, Harriett M. Mays, Kevin M. McCarthy, Carlee T. Mc-
Clendon, Eleanor R. McColl, Azile M. McCoy, Henry Bacon Mc-
Coy, Raven Ioor McDavid, Petrona R. McIver, Jean Brabham
McKinney, Stephen E. Meats, Chapman J. Milling, James Strong
Moffatt, Jr., Elizabeth F. Moore, John Fripp Morrall, Herbert A.
Moses, Bobby G. Moss, Chalmers S. Murray, Glen W. Naves,
Francis Henry Neuffer, Rene L. Neuffer, Edward F. Nolan, Joyce
S. O'Bannon, J. D. O'Bryan, Raymond K. O'Cain, James Oliphant,
Mary C. Simms Oliphant, Ruby M. Ott, Mary Celestia Parler,
Bruce L. Pearson, Virginia Pender, H. S. Petrea, A. L. Pickens,
Paul Quattlebaum, Frank H. Ramsey, Nell Peterkin Reid, T. W.
Reynolds, Monroe Ridgill, J. Kinloch Rivers, Lynn C. Robinson,
Jean Marie Rough, Archibald Rutledge, Jr., A. S. Salley, Hemrick
Salley, Mary R. Simons, Sedgwick L. Simons, John Gettys Smith,
E. D. Sloan, Vera Smith Spears, Nelle McMaster Sprott, Sarah
Cain Spruill, Paul Stevens, Samuel Gaillard Stoney, Elsie Rast
Stuart, Beatrice J. Stubbs, Thomas M. Stubbs, David Herbert
Sullivan, Iris Teal, Albert S. Thomas, Charles E. Thomas, Mar-

guerite Tolbert, Martha E. Tunander, T. Mark Verdery, Gilbert
P. Voight, W. Yeaton Wagener, David J. Watson, Ellen B. Wat-
son, Harry L. Watson, Louise M. Watson, George E. Welborn,
John R. Welsh, Jeffrey Wiles, Horace G. Williams, Jerome Wilson,
T. E. Wilson, L. S. Wolfe, Grace McBrayer Wood, Gertrude B.
Woods, John A. Zeigler, and a few others without whose help this
book could have been finished in half the time.

January 19, 1983   CLAUDE and IRENE NEUFFER
Columbia, SC

Abbeville
AB-vul, AB-bi-VIL

Natives almost swallow the second syllable of their three-syllable
town name. The second pronunciation is used by newcomers and
outsiders. Abbeville is the name of the county and of the county
seat on SC 72 between Greenwood and Calhoun Falls. Settled by
French Huguenots under the leadership of Jean Louis Gibert, it
was named (about 1790) by Dr. John de la Howe, supposedly for
his native town of Abbeville, France. Abbeville was the home of
John C. Calhoun and Major Thomas D. Howie, the "Major of St.
Lo," whose troops drove the Germans from this French city in
World War II. Site of the first county secession meeting in the
state, Abbeville was also the site of the last meeting of the Confederate Cabinet, held at the home of Major Armistead Burt, now
the residence of Mrs. Mary Stark Davis. In 1902 the G. A. Neuffer
home was built on the back lot purchased from the Starks. As a
boy, Claude Neuffer first became a gardener from digging for the
Confederate gold reputedly buried in Major Burt's "back forty."
Over the years he's grown some mighty good okra, but so far no
Confederate gold.

Acline
AE-KLINE

Acline is not a family name. One of the busiest streets in the Peedee town of Lake City (US 52 off US 378) Acline Street was
named from a blend of Atlantic Coastline, the name of the railroad it paralleled at the time. Though the railroad is now Seaboard Coastline, the street name is still Acline. Each year on the
last weekend in July Acline and all other streets in Lake City are
filled with thousands of visitors for the Tobacco Festival. Not the
least of the varied activities is the tobacco-spitting contest.

Aimar
AE-mah

Originally Adhemar, the Aimar family was one of the many Santo
Domingan French who refugeed to Charleston after the 1793
slave rebellion. Most of the families had been and continued to
be Roman Catholic. Miss Caroline Aimar writes, "Mixed marriages between Protestants and Catholics were discouraged; the
Carolina Irish were incompatible; so among themselves they spoke
French, intermarried, or just let their names die out, but they died
out in French!" The G. W. Aimar Company drugstore (1852–
1978) in Charleston at King and Vanderhorst streets was the oldest pharmacy in the same family on the same site in the South.
The founder's grandnephews, George W. and Harold A. Aimar,
were the last of the family to so serve Charleston. Their sister,
Caroline Picault Aimar, is a poet and writer of juvenile fiction
(*Waymond the Whale*, Prentice-Hall, 1975).

Alcolu
AL-cuh-LOO (OO as in boot)

This town in Clarendon County (US 521) is southeast of Sumter
and five miles northwest of Manning. Alcolu grew up around the
saw mill established in 1885 by David Wells Alderman. He con-

cocted the town's name from the first two letters of the names of
each of the three persons associated with his mill: Al from Alderman, co from Mr. Colwell, who was a partner or employee, and
lu from Lula, who was Mrs. Alderman. The town was officially
named Alcolu in 1887.

Alewine
ALE-li-WINE, AL-WINE

The pronunciation of the name varies, even among cousins. Of
German origin, the Alewine family lived in the upcountry Anderson and Abbeville area in the early half of the twentieth century
and gave their name the three-syllable pronunciation. In 1982
there were eight Alewine listings in the Greater Columbia telephone directory, some from the upcountry family and others more
recent comers to the state; both pronunciations are represented.

Allston, Alston
AWL-stun

The family names Allston and Alston are pronounced the same
in these parts, although the spelling with two l's is much more
prevalent, especially in the lowcountry. Lemuel J. Alston in 1788
owned some 11,000 acres in the upcountry along the Reedy River.
Probably the largest landowner in Greenville County, he drew
up the plat and named the village of Pleasantburg (now the center of the present city of Greenville). In 1837 William J. Alston
was president of the Jefferson-Monticello Society in the Midlands'
Winnsboro area. Allston Creek is in the Murrell's Inlet section of
Georgetown County. The now famous Brookgreen Gardens and
Forlorn Hope are among the Allston family plantations, dating
back to pre-Revolutionary John Allston. Between 1777 and 1858
nine Allstons represented five different areas of the state as representatives, senators, and governor. The artist, Washington Allston,
was born in 1779 at Brookgreen. Susan Lowndes Allston, author
of *Brookgreen Waccamaw* (1936), furnished us with the family
recipe for the classic dish, Hoppin' John: two cups of cow peas

(Carolina red peas), one cup of rice, one smoked hog jowl (here pronounced JOLE). Cover peas with cold water and boil till tender; then add jowl and boil. When jowl is tender, take it out and add rice to liquid (here called pot likker) and peas. There should be two cups of liquid to boil the rice in. When done, place peas and rice on platter. Having skinned and browned the jowl, cut in pieces, place on top of peas and rice, and serve. On New Year's Day, served along with collard greens, the peas are for good luck and the collards for greenbacks. Even if you're not superstitious, together with Awendaw cornbread it's good plain eating after the Christmas season of too much rich food.

Amaker, Amacher
AM-uh-kuh

The name is sometimes mispronounced AH-MAKE-uh. Amaker Drive in West Columbia has an Amaker family living thereon. The family is still prevalent in the Orangeburg and Dutch Fork areas. According to Mrs. Katherine Amaker Jennings, her German Swiss immigrant forebear secured a grant of land in the Orangeburg area about 1740, and his real name, still unknown to her, was incorrectly recorded as the Swiss canton from whence he came, Am-Aker. Zimmerman, Jennings, and Keitt families are among the many who claim this Amaker as a forebear.

Amick
AE-MIK

Amick is a Dutch Fork family name of German origin, originally spelled Oehmig. Some genealogists suggest Amick was originally the same name as Amaker. The name is still prevalent in the Midlands. Daniel Ernest Amick of Chapin (US 76, off I 26, northwest of Columbia) represented Lexington County in both the state House of Representatives and the Senate, 1920–1926.

Antreville
AN-tri-VIL

When you know it's located near the first upcountry Huguenot settlement, you might be tempted to look for its origin in a French family name. But its present name resulted from poor handwriting; on SC 28, eleven miles northwest of Abbeville en route to Anderson, Antreville was apparently named Centreville. Reputedly, some recorder misread the name Centreville and wrote the run-together Ce as an A. Thereafter the town was officially Antreville. Centreville was originally the home of Colonel Elias Earle from Greenville, built on land given to him for his service in the Revolution. He named it not for its central location between the two towns of Anderson and Townville (Abbeville), but for his family home in Centreville, Maryland.

Arcadia
ah-KAE-di-uh

Arcadia—from Greek mythology, referring to a peaceful, pastoral countryside—has long been used for community names all over the state. It's the name of a post office and voting precinct in upcountry Spartanburg County, a Peedee town in lower Marlboro County, a North Trenholm suburb and road in northeast Columbia, and Dr. Isaac E. Emerson's Waccamaw hunting preserve in coastal Georgetown County.

Ariail
AE-ri-uhl

The Ariaille family (now Ariail) came to South Carolina from France by way of Massachusetts. Ariail is a little Pickens County community on SC 8, west of Greenville and Easley. When its post office was closed in 1973, Robert L. Ariail tried to secure by purchase or gift the last-used post office cancelling stamp of his family-named town. But the response, "It's government property," and related bureaucratic red tape prevented the exchange, and Robert bemoaned, "Alas, my great-great-grandfather's town is now just another zip code, 29640." There are misspelled place names related to the Ariail family. The name of Mount Ariel commemorates neither the poet Shelley nor the good spirit of Shakespeare's *Tempest*, but the Ariail family. It was a post office in Greenwood County from 1825 to 1838, when its name was changed to Cokesbury. That area was also the site of Payne Institute (1870–1880), named for Bishop Daniel Alexander Payne of the African Methodist Episcopal Church; this black college was moved to Columbia in 1880 and named Allen University for A.M.E. Bishop Richard Allen. Rial Hill (pronounced RIE-uhl) was on the Ariail family land in Pickens County between Easley and Pickens, its name being a Scotch-Irish corruption of the French Ariaille. Ariel Crossroads is at the intersection of US 501 and SC 41 in the Peedee area between Gallivants Ferry and Rains. It was reputedly named for Methodist minister Luke Ariail of Mullins, who served several churches thereabouts in the 1880s. The Reverend Luke was father of Columbia College's late beloved English professor, J. Milton Ariail.

Ashepoo

ASH-i-POO (OO as in boot)

Ashepoo is an Indian word which may mean eel. Appropriately, the Ashepoo River is curling and narrow. Between the Combahee and Edisto rivers in Colleton County, the Ashepoo empties into St. Helena Sound near Beaufort. The lowcountry town of Ashepoo is on US 17, west of Jacksonboro.

Awendaw

AW-wen-DAW

This Indian word may mean deer or gun meat; hunting in the area was good. In 1701 John Lawson came through the area and wrote of the deserted Indian village there as Avendaugh-bough. The area was gradually inhabited by white settlers, and the name was spelled many different ways until the federal government assigned it a post office and legalized Awendaw. The present town is on US 17 (called the King's Highway) near Sewee River (sometimes called Awendaw Creek) about eight miles west of McClellanville. On rich bottom land, Awendaw is the corn capital of Christ Church Parish, though the yield is not always used for the famed Awendaw cornbread (some even report their crop yield as so many gallons per acre). Clemson boys of the 1930s would come back to the hills from a weekend in the lowcountry with homemade Awendaw "rye" in an oldtime fruit jar. The recipe for Awendaw "rye" is probably long-forgotten, but the recipe for Awendaw cornbread can be shared: 2 teacups of cooked hominy (grits to outsiders), 1 tablespoon of butter, ½ pint of corn meal, 4 eggs, 1 pint of milk. Mix butter with hot hominy. Beat eggs and stir into hominy. Add the milk, mixing well. Next stir in the corn meal thoroughly. The batter should be of fluid consistency; if too stiff, add a little more milk. Bake in a deep, greased pan; it will rise. Have oven at slow, steady heat, and bake about an hour. The only hitch for us city dwellers is that Mrs. Petrona McIver, Awendaw historian who gave us the recipe, warned, "None of the ingredients should be store-bought."

Bachman

BAK-mun

Though some may deem the name more properly and Germanically pronounced BAHK-mun, the renowned naturalist and Audubon collaborator, John Bachman, and all his descendants in the state have always pronounced it BAK-mun. For over 50 years he was pastor of South Carolina's oldest Lutheran Church, St. John's of Charleston, still often called John Bachman's Church. The thoroughfare there was appropriately called Dutch Church Alley until it was widened and re-named Clifford Street. Born in New York State, Doctor Bachman early came South for his health and became an ardent Southerner, offering the opening prayer of the state Secession Convention in Charleston, December 20, 1860. During his ministry Bachman tutored and prepared for the clergy three black men: Boston Drayton, John Jones, and Daniel A.

Payne. Payne later became a bishop in the African Methodist Episcopal Church. The Bachman Warbler and the Bachman Sparrow were named for his collaborator by John James Audubon, whose two sons married Bachman daughters. Bachman's name is mentioned for his assistance 134 times in Audubon's *Ornithological Biography of Birds of America*. It was through Bachman's influence that South Carolina College (University of South Carolina) was one of the three colleges in the nation (Harvard and Columbia being the other two) to order the first edition of Audubon's *Birds of America*, 1838. Bachman is credited with editing and writing substantial portions of Audubon's *The Viviparous Quadrupeds of North America*. Bachman descendants in the state include Haskells, Porchers, Roses, Chisholms, and many other prominent families, but none with the Bachman or Audubon surnames. Both Bachman-Audubon marriages produced no sons.

Bacot

buh-KOTE

Of French origin, the Bacot family is found, among other areas of the state, in the Peedee around Darlington. Here was the family plantation Belle Acres. The stream running through the section preserves the name, now corrupted through folk etymology to Belly Ache Creek. Contrary to ex post facto explanations, it is not called that because the mineral water therein might give the consumer a stomach cramp. In the early nineteenth century Pierre Bacot of the midlands' Winnsboro (US 321 and SC 213) had his home on Liberty and Fraser streets—the latter named for his mother, Bessie Fraser Bacot, whose sister was a princess, married to the second son of the King of Naples.

Banksia

BANGK-shuh

Banksia Hall is the residence of the Dan M. Hartley family. The oldest house in Barnwell (built about 1800), it was headquarters for federal occupation troops, 1865–1869. In many localities of the state, Bankshire and Bankus are names given the Lady Banksia Rose (*Rosa banksiae*), a thick-vined climber with yellow blossoms found on many a wall and fence.

Barhamville

BA-rum-VIL

Barhamville Female Institute (1828–1866) was in Richland County just north of Columbia off US 1. Dr. Elias Marks founded this famous boarding school, and later under Madame Sophie Sosnowski its gifted faculty continued giving instruction, specializing in literature and music. Among its students from all over the United States was Theodore Roosevelt's mother. The academy was named for Marks's wife Jane Barham, who had died in 1827. A road in Columbia is still called Barhamville, and the family name Barham survives, especially in Florence and Columbia.

Barnwell

BAHRN-wuhl

The present Barnwell County (part of old Winton District) and the town (US 278 and SC 70, along the Salkehatchie River) are named for the brothers John (1748–1799) and Robert (1761–1814) Barnwell, who were prominent in the Revolution and the early years of our state government. Their grandfather, Colonel John Barnwell ("Tuscarora Jack"; 1671–1724) was an Indian fighter in Colonial times. The Barnwell family continues to be prominent in varied activities. "The Barnwell Ring" in mid-twentieth-century South Carolina politics included Senator Edgar Allen Brown, House Speaker Solomon Blatt, and other Barnwell legislators. They were considered the leaders of the state legislature and therefore of the state. *The Bishop from Barnwell* by William D. Workman is a biography of Senator Brown.

Baton Rouge
BAT-un-ROOZH (OO as in booze)

This community in Chester County, north of Columbia and Fair-field County, dates from Colonial times. The French settlers used a red line to separate their land from the Indians', and thence came the name Baton Rouge—French for Red Stick.

Bayley
BAE-li

The Bayley Barony of Hilton Head Island was owned by John Bayley of Balinclough in Ireland. The present family name Bailey survives. Though Dolphin Head, the promontory overlooking Port Royal Sound, was early called Balinclough, it was not part of the Bayley Barony.

Baynard
BAE-nud

Prior to 1790 Thomas and William Baynard owned land on Edisto Island, where the native blacks pronounce the name BIN-yud. In 1790 the two Baynards bought Spanish Wells Plantation on Hilton Head Island. Thomas' son William Eddings Baynard (1800–1849) erected the imposing Baynard Mausoleum, which still stands at Zion Chapel of Ease, an Episcopal church, at the head of Broad Creek. Tradition holds that William won the thousand-acre Braddock's Point Plantation in a poker game.

Beadon
BEED-un

Bedon's Alley, running north and south for one block between Elliott and Tradd streets, is "proper" residential Charleston. (Reputedly, Charleston is the only city in the United States where you can live in an alley and be respected.) George Beadon was a member of William Sayle's colony at Old Town (Albemarle Point). George's son Henry Beadon gave his name to the alley where he owned property. The family had been landowners in Devon, England. The name appears in records as Beaudin, Beaudyn, Beadyn, Beadon, and Bedon. Richard Stobo Bedon served in the state House and Senate (1844–1854) from St. George, Dorchester County.

Beale

BEEL, BEL

The oldest house in Calhoun Falls (SC 81 and SC 72) in upcountry Abbeville County was built by Granville Beale from Massachusetts, who married a Calhoun heir. The name survives, pronounced both ways and sometimes also spelled Beall (pronounced BEL), as with Billy and Sally Beall of Lexington County. Carlisle Beall was an outstanding University of South Carolina football player of the early 1930s.

Beaty, Beattie, Beatty

BATE-i

Some few may pronounce it BEET-i, but BATE-i is heard more often. Beaty's Grist Mill in the northeast of upcountry Abbeville District was located either on Little River or on Hogskin Creek. Five legislators of the name (spelled Beattie and Beaty) represented Horry, Kershaw, and York counties in the years 1835–1918.

Beaufain

buh-FANE

The street in Charleston was named for Hector Beranger de Beaufain, colonial collector of customs and member of His Majesty's Council.

Beaufort

BUE-fuht, BOE-fuht (first pronunciation in South Carolina; second pronunciation in North Carolina)

The Duke of Beaufort was a later Lord Proprietor (being invested in the proprietorship of Lord Granville in 1709). Besides the more recently named Beaufort streets and drives throughout the state, the southeast coastal area includes a district, county, town, river, and archipelago each named for the duke. The Beaufort section is often termed "the most discovered area in the United States"—having been discovered by Spanish, French, Scots, and English, in that order, with the English settlement surviving the colonial hardships. The source of confusion for newcomers is that up the coast and across the state line the North Carolina town of Beaufort is pronounced BOE-fuht. Which is right? Both are.

Beauregard

BOE-ri-GAHD

After the BUE pronunciation for Beaufort, South Carolinians' inconsistency is evident in the BOE for Beauregard. The fort on Port Royal Island on the southeast coast is named for Confederate General Pierre Gustave Toutant Beauregard, who was in charge of the defense of the South Carolina coast. Havilah Babcock's only novel, *The Education of Pretty Boy* (1964), about an English setter named Bo, was inspired by our own gun-shy English setter, Beauregard. Our Bo's replacement, Jeb, is named for Confederate General J. E. B. Stuart of Yellow Tavern fame.

Bedenbaugh

BEE-den-BAW

Of Germanic origin, the Bedenbaugh family settled in the Dutch Fork area between the Saluda and Broad rivers. The name is still prevalent there, especially in Lexington and Newberry counties. Adam Bedenbaugh (1760–1829) was an early settler. John Benjamin Bedenbaugh, clergyman, in 1962 was a professor at Lutheran Seminary in Columbia. Jacob Moody Bedenbaugh was a surveyor, school principal, and postmaster at Prosperity.

Begin
BEG-in

Old Begin Swamp is today the site of the village of Pinopolis, off SC 6 on the neck at the southeast end of Lake Moultrie, near Monck's Corner in Berkeley County. It has also been recorded in official documents as Biggin Swamp. There was a Biggin Church (Anglican) there in 1710 between Wadboo and Biggin creeks. The church and creek are named for Biggin Hill in London.

Belin
BLANE

Cleland Belin (1792–1868) was a wealthy merchant and businessman in Willtown of Williamsburg County. In 1842–1843 he supervised the building of Black Mingo Baptist Church; known locally as Old Belin's, it was the parent of the present Nesmith Baptist Church in the nearby town of Nesmith (off SC 261, east of Kingstree). Belin was the name of the now extinct village in this same vicinity. The Belin family name today is present on Sandy Island and in Georgetown County. Belin Methodist Church is in the Myrtle Beach area of the Grand Strand.

Belly Ache
BEL-i-AKE

When you consider that the stream's original name was Belle Acres Creek, it becomes clear that the present Belly Ache Creek is not a description but an accepted mispronunciation. The stream in Darlington County is not named because its mineral waters might cause stomach cramps; it runs through the old Bacot family plantation, Belle Acres, and by folk etymology (continued mis-pronunciation) its present name evolved.

Beresford
BEHRZ-fud

Beresford Alley and Beresford Street in Charleston are no more. They were named for colonial landowners John and Richard Beresford. By city ordinance in 1805 Beresford Alley, between Meeting and Church streets, combined with and took the name of Chalmers Alley, today the bumpy cobblestoned Chalmers Street. Over 100 years later, again by city ordinance, Beresford Street became Fulton Street; the city fathers had eliminated the Big Brick, the famous house of prostitution on Beresford, and decided—because of its unsavory association—the name Beresford also had to go. (See Horry.)

Berkeley
BUHRK-li

In England the name is pronounced BAHRK-li, as in Berkeley Square, but in South Carolina it is pronounced more phonetically. Lowcountry Berkeley County on the Cooper River and around Lake Moultrie is named for two Lords Proprietors, Lord John Berkeley and Sir William Berkeley. Here, in the eastern part of the county, is the noted and notorious Hell Hole Swamp—noted as one of General Francis Marion's hideouts during the Revolution; notorious for its exportation of corn liquor to New York and elsewhere during the sad days when the infamous Eighteenth Amendment was part of the Constitution. The Hell Hole Swamp Festival, held annually the first weekend in May in the little town of Jamestown (US 17A and SC 45) on the Santee River, features whiskeymaking exhibits, a reptile show, grits-grinding, and quilting.

Betaw

BEE-taw

It's an Indian word that may mean honeybee or alligator. Betaw Plantation on the Santee River was the home of Samuel Peyre Thomas and his Huguenot forebears, the Peyres. A later descendant, John Peyre Thomas, Columbia attorney and dean of the University of South Carolina Law School, named his Myrtle Beach front-row summer home Betaw. The site has now been gobbled up by the Grand Strand's carnival area.

Bethea

buh-THAE

One present Bethea says he's French Huguenot, another says English, and Bethia is Scottish, but they all pronounce the name buh-THAE. Preston Land Bethea (1870–1944), teacher and farmer, served in the state House and Senate from Marion (now Dillon) County. The section of Dillon County known as The Skillet has been owned for over 100 years by the family of Dennis Bethea, a slave who, when freed, was given the land by his former master, Will Bethea.

Blatt

BLOT

Solomon Blatt (born 1896), Barnwell lawyer and longtime member of the state legislature, served as Speaker of the House for 25 years and is still an influential member. He is the only survivor of the politically powerful group known as "the Barnwell Ring," which included Edgar Allen Brown, J. Emile Harley, and Winchester Smith.

Blenheim
BLEN-um

At the intersection of SC 381 and SC 38, this little Peedee town in Marlboro County was first known as Mineral Spring; when the post office was established it was called Three Creeks. In 1882 the area was incorporated and Donald Matheson gave it the present name Blenheim, for Castle Blenheim, the home of the Duke of Marlborough, for whom the county is named.

Bobo
BOE-BOE

The prosperous Union County Bobo family gave its name to a ford and some of its family tradition to a house name. The Cross Key House, twelve miles southwest of Union at the intersection of Old Buncombe Road and Old Ninety Six Road, was built in 1812–1814 by Barrum Bobo. The house, at the center of a large plantation during the antebellum period, has a date stone with the original owner's initials, B.B., 1814, and a pair of crossed keys— Bobo is reputed to have been a ship's purser, the keeper of the keys. The nearby town is named Cross Keys (SC 49). Five miles west in Spartanburg County is the town of Cross Anchor. It is reputedly named for the house (burned in 1932) built by the former captain of the British ship *Salley*, on which Barrum Bobo had been the purser. Though the captain's name is not known, the family name of the purser, Bobo, still survives in the area.

Bodenheimer, Bodenhamer
BODE-un-HIE-muh, BODE-un-HAE-muh

Several Bodenheimers were late German immigrants to North Carolina, more recently come to the Columbia area. One branch of the family began a business that involved barrel packing, but their name was one letter too long for the label to be used on the barrel; so they changed their name to Bodenhamer (BODE-un-HAE-muh).

Bodie, Boddie
BOD-i

The family in the Midlands around Batesburg (US 1 and US 178) came from England via North Carolina. The handed-down story in the Bodie family is that they were successful pirates on the Atlantic seaboard. In a bad storm they were shipwrecked off the North Carolina coast in the Nag's Head–Cape Hatteras area. Those who made it to shore settled on the island that still bears the family name. The sign there, "Bodie's Island Lighthouse," adds just below, "pronounced Body." Professor Edward Bodie is a member of the English Department faculty of the University of South Carolina. Dr. U. Hoyt Bodie (who told us the pirate story) serves in the Department of Radiology and Nuclear Medicine at South Carolina Baptist Hospital. Back in the 1960s Mark Bodie was a slugger in Forest Little League out at Columbia's Satchel Ford School. The family name Boddie, perhaps a phonetic spelling of Bodie, is also present in the state. William Willis Boddie is author of *History of Williamsburg County* (1923).

Boineau
BOI-NOE (OI as in noise)

Like Bonneau (which might have been the same name at one time), Boineau is French Huguenot and is still present as a family name in the Midlands. In 1961 Charles E. Boineau of Columbia was the first Republican elected to the state legislature since Reconstruction. Today, with our Republican legislators, congressmen, and United States senator, the Grand Old Party has come "a fur piece" since that day in Charleston back in the 1930s when traffic was backed up in all four directions at Meeting and Broad streets while Cornelia Dabney Tucker strolled through the intersection. An amazed visiting motorist asked the cop on the corner, "Do you always stop traffic this way for a lady to cross?" And the policeman explained, "Suh, that's not just a lady. That's the whole state Republican party!"

Bonham

BONE-um

The Columbia street in Shandon is rapidly becoming accepted as BON-um—maybe a prettier sound, but Milledge L. Bonham (governor, 1862–1864) and his family have always answered to BONE-um. In front of Bonham's old home in Abbeville District near Troy (now in Greenwood County) is Flat Grove Cemetery, burial place for Bonhams, Butlers, and Smiths. The Bonham family is still present in nearby Anderson County.

Bonneau

buh-NOE

The French Huguenot family gave its name to a ferry, beach, and town in lowcountry Berkeley County on US 52, east of Lake Moultrie. Bonneau might originally have been the same name as the slightly different Boineau. Peter Porcher Bonneau of Laurel Hill Plantation was a state senator (1856–1860) and a surgeon in the Civil War. In 1867 G. W. DeHay was postmaster of Bonneau.

Bordeaux

bohr-DOE

The town of New Bordeaux in old Abbeville District was the first Huguenot settlement (1764) in the upcountry. Bordeaux—no longer called New—is off SC 81 in McCormick County en route to Clark Hill Reservoir. Evidencing the sometimes lost *r* in Southern speech, one storekeeper in the town explained, "Some people hereabouts call it BUHRD-DOE, but it's really BOE-DOE." Her forbidden pronunciation was compatible with her sale of "Sunday milkshakes"—that's a euphemism for beer sold on the seventh day, contrary to South Carolina's variegated blue laws.

Borough
BUH-ruh

Borough House was the only residence in pre-Revolutionary Stateburg (SC 261, just north of US 378) when the town was first established in Sumter County, east of Columbia. Locally called Anderson House, then Hill Crest, the old home is now given its original name, Borough House, and is occupied by the initial owner's descendant, Captain R. K. Anderson. Like the Church of the Holy Cross just across the road, Borough House is built of pise de terre (rammed earth).

Bouknight
BAWK-nite

The family name, also spelled Bauknight, was originally the German Bauknecht. The family settled in the Dutch Fork area of the Midlands before the Revolution. Bauknight Ferry in Newberry County was the scene of a skirmish (1782) in the Revolution. In the 1982 Greater Columbia telephone directory there are over 125 listings of Bouknight and 16 of Bauknight. Dr. Joseph W. Bouknight, distinguished professor emeritus, was for 40 years on the chemistry faculty of the University of South Carolina. The many-branched Palmetto Hardware stores in the Midlands were established by Manning Bauknight and his brother, retired Colonel Ralph Bauknight of Ballentine.

Boulware
BOLE-uh (like one who bowls)

Thomas McCullough Boulware in 1860 was the largest slave owner in old Chester District with 157 slaves. His handsome home in Blackstock (off US 321 north of Columbia) was burned by General William T. Sherman in 1865. The Boulware family is still prominent in the Midlands, especially in Fairfield County. Harold Boulware, one of the state's first black attorneys, is now a judge in Columbia.

Bowie
BOO-i (rhymes with chewy)

The first Bowies in old Abbeville District were pre-Revolutionary settlers. Major John Bowie served throughout the Revolution. His sons George and Alexander were prominent lawyers; Alexander went to Alabama, where he served as chancellor and trustee of the University of Alabama. This family of Bowies were members of Upper Long Cane Creek Presbyterian Church, the oldest church (established in 1763) in Abbeville County. Later, other Bowies, descended from Abraham Bowie of Scotland, came to Maryland about 1700, and then to Abbeville District about 1800. In 1817 Eli Bowie established Gilgal Methodist Church in the Buckstand section, where the annual Bowie family reunion is still held.

Bram
BRAHM

Bram's Point on Hilton Head Island may owe its sophisticated *ah* sound to its possible namesake William Gerard DeBrahm (1717–about 1799), surveyor, who made the first map of South Carolina and Georgia (1757) and fortified the city of Charleston (1755).

bream
BRIM

This prolific little freshwater fish is one which sportscasters too often call BREEM. No South Carolinian, man or boy, ever went BREEM fishing; as writer-hunter-fisherman Havilah Babcock observed, "Any boy big enough to button his britches knows it's BRIM, not BREEM." Yates Snowden agreed, judging from his rhyme scheme in this passage from "A Carolina Bourbon":

> And here was mooted many a day,
> The question on which each gourmet

> Throughout the parish had his say;
>> Which is best,
> Santee or Cooper River bream?
> Alas! The evening star grew dim,
> Ere any guest agreed with him,
> Or he with guest.

It took many years to persuade the dictionary fellows that since it's our fish, our pronunciation should be included in the dictionaries. Now BRIM is recorded in most of them as "provincial pronunciation."

Brennecke
BREN-ni-ki

It's a German family name in the northwest Walhalla area (SC 107 and SC 183) of Oconee County. Marguerite Brennecke contributed some of our earliest notes on names in her native heath to *Names in South Carolina*.

Brogdon
BROG-dun

Bearing the family name of early settlers there, the town of Brogdon is on US 521 southeast of the county seat of Sumter. John Brogdon Memorial School, eight miles south of Sumter on the Manning Road, was named for the founder and first pastor of Graham Baptist Church. The one-teacher school on Brogdon Siding is no more, but one item from the little school remains in a Brogdon family home: the bench on which the girls used to sit.

Broughton
BRAWT-uhn

The Broughtons were a Colonial family in Orangeburg District (south of Columbia). Bruton's Fork, north of Bennettsville in

Marlboro County, was probably named for Wiliby Broughton. He owned practically all the land at the fork of Beaver Dam and Crooked Creek. But even with all that space, he felt cramped; in order to move west he reputedly traded all his land to James Stubbs for a horse, a saddle, a bridle, and a rifle. In 1837 James Stubbs donated land for Bruton's Fork Baptist Church. The Broughton name, from other forebears, still survives in the state.

Bruckmout

BRUK-mowt

Bruckmout Gutter on Edisto Island is a Gullah name for one of the narrow saltwater drains (dry at low tide) that interlace the marshes. A gutter is a drain; bruckmout is Gullah for broad mouth. Other less wide gutters on Edisto are called Mellisham (Mellichamp) Bay and John Brown.

Buncombe

BUNGK-um

Lowcountry Buncombe Plantation in Clarendon County near the town of Summerton along Nelson Ferry Road was first owned by Dr. Thomas Leslie Burgess. Farther upcountry in Edgefield and in Greenville there are highways named Buncombe Road, possibly because they lead to Buncombe County, North Carolina, of which Asheville is the county seat. A Congressman from that area made his county famous and possibly contributed a new meaning for the word. In Congress he frequently rose to pontificate, "I must speak in behalf of my noble constituents of Buncombe County. . . ." The groans could be heard throughout the hall of the House, and the expression, "a lot of buncombe," came into being, meaning baloney, hogwash, or much ado about nothing.

Burroughs
BUH-ruhz

Burroughs is a prominent family name in coastal Horry County; the family had originally settled at Snow Hill on Waccamaw Lake. Franklin G. Burroughs, in *The Independent Republic* (Spring 1981), wrote delightfully of his roots and residence, warning that he had done very little research so that, if his account "should be read at some future date, a generous supply of salt should be kept handy."

Buyck
BIKE

Some are tempted to pronounce two syllables, BUE-ik, like the car, but in South Carolina the family name is just one, BIKE. Mark W. Buyck, Jr., is a Florence lawyer and former United States District Attorney. In the Midlands, Buyck Bottom Creek is a tributary of Butler's Gut Creek in Calhoun County, where also is located Preference Farm, home of Peter Buyck.

Buzzard
buh-ZAHRD

Some members of the family of early German settlers have kept the original spelling of their name—Bushardt (BOOSH-ahrt; OO as in foot). Others have accepted various spellings, including Buzzard, with the second syllable accented.

Bynum
BIE-num

Bynum Street was the name for the slave quarters of Bynum Plantation on the Old Camden Road near Wateree Swamp, a plantation previously owned by Mathew Richard Singleton. Nathaniel F. Bynum was one of the owners of Nutshell Plantation in lower Richland County. The Bynum cemetery is just east of the Nutshell house. Members of the Seay family are also buried there. In 1803 John Bynum of Richland County was made surveyor general of the state. And well-known for a brief time was a literary Bynum: he published one volume of poetry; he edited one newspaper; he fought and lost one duel—such was the brief career of Turner Bynum, Jr. His father ran a store on Columbia's Main Street in 1815. Soon after the publication of his little volume of romantic poetry, young Turner was hired by the Nullifiers to edit a newspaper in Greenville to combat Benjamin F. Perry's anti-Nullification journal. Bynum's editorials resulted in a duel challenge from Perry and in Bynum's death from the bullet wound in 1829. Perry later became governor of the state. Clarke Bynum of Wilson Hall Academy in Sumter was elected to the National High School Coaches' All-American Basketball Team in 1980.

Cades

KADEZ (one syllable; rhymes with raids)

The unincorporated town of Cades (SC 512, east of US 52) is in Williamsburg County north of Kingstree. Named for the Cade family there, it was originally called Camp Branch; General Francis Marion camped there in 1780 on his way to Tarcote, in the fork of the Black River, to seize British supplies. Former Governor Robert E. McNair was born in Cades. Guilford Cade was a notable twentieth-century planter in upcountry Abbeville County. A graduate of University of the South at Sewanee, he held annual barbecues for all the people on his land and his kin and friends in the neighborhood. Planter Cade also ran the family mill on Little River, which had been built by John Louis Gibert, namesake and grandnephew of the leader of the first upcountry Huguenot settlement (1764).

Cahusac

kuh-ZAK

This French Huguenot family name was well-known in early St. Stephen's and St. John's Berkeley. Peter Cahusack married Mary Mauzequen 18 June 1749.

Calais

kuh-LAE

In coastal Carolina a town, landing, tavern, and plantation have had this French name. Calais Plantation was named before the Revolution by Henry Laurens for the French city on the English Channel. The plantation is at the narrowest point on the north side of Winyah Bay in Georgetown County. As with the two European cities opposite each other across the Channel, across Winyah Bay from Calais Plantation is Dover Plantation. They long were crossing points for early travelers. The Calais-Dover Ferry over Ityone (Etiwan) River, now called Cooper River, was vested in John Clement in 1785.

Calcott

KAHL-kut

A recent visitor to Columbia's University of South Carolina campus asked the location of the KAHL-kut Building. After she'd twice had to repeat the name, the student at the information desk incorrectly corrected her, "Oh, you mean the KAL-KOT Building." He did know that the Calcott Building faces Bull Street and is right behind Russell House. They were both in a hurry; she just thanked him; so he still doesn't know that it's KAHL-kut, named for Wilfred Calcott, a professor she and a host of other students had for Latin-American history back in the early 1940s.

Calhoun

KAL-HOON, kul-HOON (OO as in booze)

Organizations, streets, and a county are named for John Caldwell Calhoun, United States Vice President, Secretary of State, U.S. Senator, and Congressman. Born in Abbeville District on Lower Long Cane Creek, John C. Calhoun entered the junior class at Yale from Dr. Moses Waddel's Academy in Willington (now in McCormick County) and was graduated from Yale with honors. Calhoun County in Texas was named in appreciation for the role Calhoun played in Texas' admission to statehood in 1845. A county and town in Georgia are also named for him. The town of Calhoun Falls, on SC 72, southwest of Abbeville and three miles from the Savannah River, is named for John's cousin, James Edward Calhoun, lawyer and owner of Millwood Plantation. Calhoun Street in Barnwell, South Carolina, is named for Harry D. Calhoun, banker and civic leader. Though the name is pronounced kul-HOON by some of the older generation, KAL-HOON is now more prevalent. The earlier spelling of the name was from the Scottish clan Colquhoun, also pronounced kul-HOON and still present in the state. Dr. Donald Colquhoun is professor of geology at the Columbia campus of the University of South Carolina.

Calibogue

KAL-i-BOE-gi

Calibogue Point, the southern tip of Hilton Head Island, is now called Braddock's Point. Calibogue Sound is the deep channel between Hilton Head Island and Daufuskie Island, just north of the Savannah River. On several early maps Calibogue Sound is recorded as Daufuski River or Daufuski Sound. The word Calibogue may be Creek Indian for deep spring, though some believe it refers to a spruce beer or hot rum drink.

Calico
KAL-i-KOE

Calico is a section in the heart of the upcountry textile industry in Spartanburg and Cherokee counties near Gaffney. Some would assume the place name is from calico cloth. Actually it is a blend of the first two letters of each of the words in the business name Campbell Limestone Company, of which William Campbell is the founder-owner.

Callibeauf
KAL-i-BUF

Charleston's Callibeauf (also spelled Callibuff) Lane was named for the man who lived there. On the original map of the town it was Middle Street, in the heart of the retail business area. After Callibeauf it was called Poinsett Lane, from Poinsett Tavern thereon, and now it is Elliott Street.

Campobello
KAMP-uh-BEL-uh

The town and polling precinct is fifteen miles north of Spartanburg on US 176 near the North Carolina line. According to legend, it was originally Campa Bella, meaning beautiful fields. Once a popular health spa for the mineral springs there, Campobello received its official name when the Spartanburg-Asheville railroad was built through the community. It was also a well-known learning center after the Baptist preacher, the Reverend I. W. Wingo, started the Monk Institute there in 1894.

Canadys
KAN-uh-DIS

The lowcountry Colleton County town on the Edisto River is at
the junction of US 15 and SC 61, and is named for the Canady
family. That family name is still present in the state, as is the
similar name Canaday.

Capers
KAE-puhz

The French Huguenot Capier family came to South Carolina by
way of Wales and England, and along the way the name was
anglicized to Capers. Capers brothers William, Richard and Gabriel, planters and schoolteachers, came to the colony about 1679.
In the nineteenth century William Capers was a bishop in the
Methodist Episcopal Church, South. His son, Ellison Capers, was
a bishop in the Episcopal Church in South Carolina. Ellison also
served as a Confederate brigadier general and was called The
Fighting Bishop.

Capstone
KAP-STONE

Though the pronunciation is obvious, we couldn't resist including
its "origin." The tallest structure on the University of South Carolina campus when it was built, Capstone is the seventeen-story
dormitory in Columbia on Barnwell Street at Gibbes Court. It's
topped with a revolving restaurant. According to a widely distributed picture postcard, the Capstone House was named for
Commodore Epaminondas J. Capstone of the Confederate Navy
—an unintentional hoax because the photographer (who wrote
the description for the postcard) accepted as fact a facetious edi-
torial in Columbia's *The State* newspaper. Editor William D.
Workman was taking the University to task for having delayed
in naming so many of its new buildings; he made up famous

alumni to fit the buildings' descriptive names: Capstone, the brothers Under and Post Graduate, Life Science, et al. Since there never was a Commodore Epaminondas J. Capstone of the Confederate Navy, the postcard (now a collector's item) has been withdrawn from circulation. The dormitory is still not officially named and is still called the Capstone or, less pompously, the Adult Merry-Go-Round.

Carolina
KA-ruh-LINE-uh

Imitaters of Southern speech to the contrary, no literate South Carolinian ever omits the second syllable and says KA-LINE-uh. The second syllable is there, very unaccented, and mayhaps not heard by those who are accustomed to a more precise (dare we say harsher?) speech and who accent the first three syllables, KA-ROE-LINE-ah. Note the line in the song, "Nothing could be finer than to be in Carolina"; KA-ruh-LINE-uh is the pronunciation that fits the rhythm of that truism.

Carteret
KAHR-tuh-RET

The name of Sir George Carteret, one of the initial Lords Proprietors, was preserved in eighteenth-century maps in Cape Carteret (now called Cape Romain—its earlier Spanish name) on the coast out from McClellanville. One of the four bastions in colonial Charleston's defense system was the Carteret. After Sir George's death (1695), he was succeeded as a lord proprietor by his son Sir John Carteret, first Earl of Granville, for whom the colonial Granville County was named and also the present Carteret Street in Beaufort.

Cashua

KASH-wuh

Cashua has been the name of a ferry, neck, church, and now a street in the Peedee area. The old ferry (at present US 52 and SC 151) was eleven miles east of the town of Darlington and has now been replaced by a bridge connecting the counties of Darlington and Marlboro. The ferryman required cash—cash-way fare—before he'd haul customers and carts across the river. Over the years Cashway Ferry became Cashua Ferry, and the name is preserved today in Cashua Street.

Cassatt

KAS-et

The little town of Cassatt in Kershaw County in the Midlands is on US 1 northeast of Camden. When the railroad was built through the area, Cassatt was named for the man who was president of the Pennsylvania Railroad and had a statue erected in his honor in New York's Pennsylvania Station.

Catawba

kuh-TAW-buh

The name has been mispronounced KAT-uh-BAW and kuh-TAH-buh. An Indian word possibly meaning cut-off or caved-in river banks, Catawba is the name of a river, an Indian tribe, one of the two chief colonial trails in South Carolina, several streets, and the last Indian reservation in the state. The Catawba Path (historian A. S. Salley said trail was a western term; and in Mississippi it's Natchez Trace for the longest path of all) followed the river valleys up from Charleston through the Midlands toward Camden (via Columbia's present Two Notch Road), and on into Chester, Lancaster, and York counties. In these three counties are the 144,000 acres the present-day Catawba Indians claim were illegally taken from them in 1840—land including the cities of Rock

Hill, Fort Mill, the Tega Cay development, and part of the Carowinds Amusement Park.

Cateechee
kuh-TEE-chee

She was a fictional Indian maid, who was so "documented" that
she now has many places named for her and some people get up-
set when we say she wasn't "for real." In the 1890s James Henry
Rice (historian and father of Carew Rice, the silhouettist) wrote
a story, set in the northwest upcountry area during the 1760 Indian War, about the Cherokee maiden Cateechee, called Isaqueena in the Choctaw language. She overheard the Indian chief
telling his braves of plans to attack Cambridge Fort (the Star
Fort at Ninety Six) the next day. Cateechee immediately left the
Cherokee town of Keowee and rode the 96 miles down to the
Star Fort and Cambridge to warn her white lover Allen Francis
and his people. As she crossed the streams on her ride down the
path, she named them—Six Mile Creek, Twelve Mile Creek,
Eighteen Mile Creek, Six and Twenty Mile Creek, etc., and these
names are still recorded on maps today. In 1898 Dr. James Walter
Daniel, Methodist minister in Abbeville, wrote the story in verse,
Cateechee of Keowee. His little book, with explanatory notes and
an introduction claiming the story to be "a historical fact," was
widely popular and much believed. When, on television or radio
talk shows, we call the Cateechee story a hoax, we get calls from
indignant folk who disagree: "We know it's true. We have Doctor Daniel's documented book. Do you dare to question the word
of a man of the cloth?" We too were among the believers until
state historian A. S. Salley showed us George Hunter's 1730 map
whereon the streams, creeks, and rivers down the old Cherokee
Path were already named, 30 years before Cateechee's ride, for
their distance from the village of Keowee—named by the traders
who traveled the trail to swap wares with the Indians. The village
of Ninety Six (without the hyphen) was also already named.
Names that commemorate the fictional maiden include Cateechee
Mill on Twelve Mile River, a brand of flour called Cateechee,
the Cateechee Daughters of the American Revolution Chapter in

Anderson, and Isaqueena Falls on the river crossed by the Cherokee Path.

Cayce

KAE-si

The town in Lexington County, across the Congaree River from
Columbia, derives its name from Cayce's Tavern there, in railroad
days called Cayce's Siding. The land, inherited by tavern keeper
James Cayce's wife, whose maiden name was Arthur, was part of
the little village of Granby (1750–1790) near Friday's Ferry.
Granby was probably named for planter Arthur's wife, whose
maiden name was Granby; the story that the village was named
for the Earl of Granby has never been documented. Now on the
National Register of Historic Places, the home of William J. Cayce
(1864–1948) on Holland Avenue at First Street was built in 1917
by the merchant for whose family the town is named. The name
Cayce is probably a respelling of a German name and not from
the Irish Casey.

Chanson

SHA-saw

It's the French word for song or poem, and we still try to pronounce it as the French do, though somewhat Carolinized. *Carolina Chansons* (1922) is the poetic volume of DuBose Heyward
and Hervey Allen, better known for *Porgy* and *Anthony Adverse*,
respectively. John Zeigler of the Charleston Book Basement back
in 1965 told us of selling his last copy of this little poetic gem to
a tourist. He didn't know how proud she was of her Southern
forebears until she commented as she left the shop, "You know,
my great-grandmother was a CHAN-sun from Charleston." Alas
for her, there is no such family name to our knowledge.

Chattooga
chuh-TOO-guh (OO as in booze)

The Chattooga River is the head stream of the Savannah on the upper boundary in Oconee County between South Carolina and Georgia. Chattooga is an Indian word possibly meaning rocky waters—attested to in recent years by many who have dared to ride the river's rapids. The river is the setting for the University of South Carolina's poet-in-residence James Dickey's novel *Deliverance*.

Chauga
CHAW-guh

The Indian word possibly means high or lifted up. Chauga is the name of a river and a Baptist church in the northwest corner of the state. Established on the Georgia side of the Tugaloo River in 1795, the church soon moved east to the Chauga River in Oconee County.

Chavous
CHAE-vis

The French Huguenot family is still found in Allendale County. Douglas Chavous, Columbia pharmacist, served several years as a winning coach of Forest Little League at Satchel Ford School. The more Anglicized name, also found in the lowcountry, is Chavis.

Cheraw
chuh-RAW

The name is often mispronounced shuh-RAW. Cheraw is an Indian word possibly meaning a signal station or look-out point to sight the approaching enemy. Appropriately the town of Cheraw is on high ground overlooking the surrounding area. In Chester-field County some fifteen miles from the North Carolina line, Cheraw (US 1 at SC 401) is the native heath of former Columbia radio talkshowman Jerry D. Pate and nationally known black jazz musician Dizzie Gillespie.

Cherokee
CHEH-ruh-KEE

From the Indian word meaning fiery or ground squirrel, Chero-kee is possibly our most prevalent Indian place name—a county in the northwestern part of the state; a colonial trail from the coast along the river valleys into the western backcountry (now Oconee County) to the Cherokee town of Keowee; a waterfall; a white rose; a voting precinct; streets and roads throughout the state; and Cherokee Springs, five miles northeast of Spartanburg on US 221, renowned for its mineral water at the turn of the century. The name Cherokee Road in Aiken (near the Savannah River) was short-lived. Originally Whiskey Road, it was so called because in early days the road, and its extensions, were used for hauling rum from the coast inland. Some summers ago the ladies of the Aiken Improvement Society changed the name Whiskey Road to Cherokee Road and appropriately planted climbing Cherokee roses along the road's borders. When the winter resi-dents—Northerners who wintered in Aiken's milder climate—re-turned to town, a veritable hullabaloo arose, and the road got back its alcoholic name. Appropriately, close to town Whiskey Road intersects with Brandy Lane, hard by Easy Street.

Chesnee
CHEZ-ni

Chesnee, a town on US 221 northeast of Spartanburg and three miles from the North Carolina line, is not named from an Indian word, despite its -ee ending. John B. Cleveland of Spartanburg, with other wealthy citizens, established Chesnee Land Company, and named it for his great-grandmother Margaret Chesnee (also spelled Chesney) of Scotland. She came to America with Mr. Cleveland's great-grandfather Alexander Vernon on his second trip to the North Tyger River area. Chesnee is now a thriving textile manufacturing community.

Cheves
CHIV-vis

Langdon Cheves (1776–1857) was born in old Abbeville District, a descendant from the Scots Chivas family. As president of the United States Bank (1819–1822), he built up reserves and saved the bank, earning the nickname "The Hercules of the U.S. Bank." Near Lancaster, Pennsylvania, on the Columbia Pike, Cheves' antebellum home, called Abbeville, where he lived for a time in the 1820s, has recently been placed on the National Register of Historic Places.

Chicora
shuh-KOH-ruh

In contrast to the Indian word Cheraw, the CH here has an SH sound. Chicora apparently means ruler and people of the tribe. Paul Quattlebaum's book *The Land Called Chicora* tells of the Indians and the land on the north coastal area, now Horry and Georgetown counties. Chicora Wood Plantation on the Peedee River was the home of pre-Civil War Governor Robert Withers Allston. His daughter, Elizabeth Waties Allston Pringle (alias Patience Pennington), wrote *Chronicles of Chicora Wood* (1922). The old town of Chicora, four miles west of Pinopolis in low-country Berkeley County, is now covered by Lake Moultrie. The land was owned by Dr. Philip G. Prioleau, then by the Porcher family, and then by New Yorker A. S. Emerson, who in about 1890 laid off lots for the town of Chicora—also called New England City. Chicora College, specializing in music, was in Columbia in the early 1930s, but moved to Charlotte to combine with Queens College. ⭑ Chicora College was in Greenville, S.C. also. Roselle Dills mother graduated from it there in 1918.

Chitterling
CHIT-lin

Cautious linguists may pronounce the three-syllable CHIT-uhr-LINGZ, but the folks that eat them just say CHIT-linz. Chitterlings are hog intestines. Thoroughly cleaned and boiled for hours, they've been used for sausage casings. Cut link-size and fried, some folks really like them. The Chit'lin Strut, a festival in the Aiken County town of Salley, has been held on the Saturday after Thanksgiving since 1966. It was first suggested by Friendly Ben Dekle, Cayce radio personality, to Salley Mayor Jack Abel as a fund raiser for the little town that needed a new fire engine. By now the Chit'lin Strut has secured Salley much more than a fire engine. Each year over 30,000 people come from all over the country to eat about 10,000 pounds of chit'lins (they don't sell 'em by the yard any more), 8,000 fried chickens, 750 barbecued pigs, and other trimmings. For entertainment there are parades, country music, horseshoe pitching, historical displays, mule rides, and dancing—the chit'lin strut, of course.

Clinton
KLIN-tun

This little town (northwest of Columbia off I 26) in Laurens County is not pronounced like the New York city (KLINT-uhn). Clinton, South Carolina, established officially in 1850, was named for Colonel Henry Clinton Young, a prominent lawyer in the county.

Clio
KLIE-OE

The town of Clio is on SC 9, southwest of Bennettsville, in Marlboro County in the northeastern part of the state known as the Peedee. Named for the muse of history, Clio was previously called Ivey's Crossroads and then Hawleyville for early merchants there.

William Rogers, who came from the North to establish a store at the crossroads, is reputed to have named the area Clio. Rogers was the maternal grandfather of former Governor Thomas G. McLeod. Mount Clio Academy, the first educational institute in Lee County, at the intersection of Bethune Road and the highway to Darlington, was chartered in 1818 in Bishopville.

Coggeshall
KOG-shul

Of English origin, the family settled in Darlington in the Peedee section. Coggeshalls are now throughout the state, but especially in the Peedee (Hartsville, Darlington, and Florence) and west of Columbia in Ballentine (US 76, off I 26).

Colcolough
KOE-kli

Also spelled Colclough, the Colcoloughs were an early Charleston family. In lowcountry Summerton (Clarendon County) J. H. Colclough is said to have built in the 1840s the home on Cantey Street now owned by the James family. The Colclough name is now present in the Midlands at Ridge Spring and Batesburg. The Venerable Frederick Colclough Byrd, Archdeacon of the Diocese of Upper South Carolina, is a native of Ridge Spring. Thomas Edward Colcolough is a mill executive in upcountry Union.

Colleton
KOL-luh-tun

Lowcountry Colleton County, of which Walterboro is the county seat, was named for Sir John Colleton, one of the three original Lords Proprietors. His share passed to his eldest son Thomas Colleton, and then to his grandson Peter Colleton; his third son James Colleton was a landgrave and governor of the Carolina province (1686–1690). On the Lords Proprietors' Map of 1672 the Ashepoo River is also called Colleton River. Colleton County is between the Edisto and Combahee rivers.

Combahee
KUM-BEE

Spelling to the contrary, Combahee has long been pronounced as two syllables by folks in these parts. It may be an Indian word meaning small risings. The Combahee River is formed by Salke-hatchie and Cuckold creeks (the second later called Chee-Ha and now Chehaw River) and flows between Colleton and Beaufort counties into St. Helena Sound. In Columbia's affluent residential area, Wales Garden (which during the Depression was called Mortgage Hill), Combahee Avenue is one of nine streets named for South Carolina Indian tribes. Although some report that the Cumbee family name, long present in the coastal village of Mc-Clellanville, is a phonetic spelling of Combahee, others report that the name dates back to Elizabethan England. The family name Cumbie may be related.

Comingtee
KUM-ming-TEE

It's neither Chinese nor Indian. The Coming family plantation was on the Cooper River thirty miles from the mouth, at the T where the river divided into its eastern and western branches. For a long time the plantation was called Coming's T (so marked on old plats), then Coming T, and now Comingtee. The original owners were John and Affra Coming. Widowed and childless, Affra left Comingtee to her nephew Elias Ball, who with his wife had come from England to help her manage the plantation. John Coming was first mate on the frigate *Carolina*, which left London for Charleston in 1669. In 1692 Coming and Thomas Smith were given power of attorney to manage the provincial affairs of the recently departed Landgrave James Colleton. Coming was long a prominent family in early Charleston, where one of the streets bears the name.

Conestee
KON-es-tee

The present upcountry town of Conestee (off US 25, south of Greenville) bears an Indian name possibly meaning dogwood. Mills Atlas (1825) does not show Conestee, but shows nearby Carruth's Armory.

Congaree
KONG-guh-REE

The Indian word meaning "scraping bottom" is an appropriate name for the sometimes too shallow, rock-laden Congaree River. Formed at Columbia by the confluence of the Broad and Saluda rivers, the Congaree flows southeast to empty into Lake Marion. The Indian tribe's name is also used for streets in towns all over the state; for the old fort (1718), the first white outpost in the Dutch Fork, across the Broad River from present Columbia; for the swamp south of Columbia (Beidler Tract in Congaree Swamp has been termed the most valuable timberland in the Southeast); and for towns in the Midlands—Congaree in Lower Richland on SC 769 between Horrell Hill and Gadsden, and South Congaree in Lexington County on SC 302 south of Columbia Metropolitan Airport.

Coogler
KOO-gluh (OO as in boot)

The German name was Kugler. J. Gordon Coogler (1865–1901) was called The Bard of the Congaree. His volumes *Purely Original Verse*, circulated annually from his little print shop on Columbia's Lady Street, added a new word to our language: a Cooglerism is a solemn absurdity, exemplified in Coogler's couplet, "Alas, for the South! Her books have grown fewer— she never was much given to literature," quoted at the beginning of H. L. Mencken's "The Sahara of the Bozart" (*Prejudices*, 1920). With the re-issue of Coogler's complete poetic works, Coogler Fan Clubs may once again flourish as in days of yore in Atlanta, Chicago, Boston, and even across the water at Cambridge University. Collateral descendants of the bard live in the Midlands' Irmo and across the Savannah River from Calhoun Falls in Elberton, Georgia.

Cooper

KOOP-uh (OO as in foot)

Though New York folk and novelist James Fenimore Cooper pronounce the name KOOP-uhr, with the OO as in booze, anywhere in South Carolina the family—except for newcomers—and place names are just as properly pronounced KOOP-uh, with the OO as in foot. Cooper River, originally given the Indian name Etiwan, and the Ashley River are named for the most prominent of the Lords Proprietors, Lord Ashley Cooper. They are two of South Carolina's few major streams without Indian names. Since they join to form the peninsula of Charleston, residents thereon—not known for their modesty—opine that Charleston is where the Ashley and Cooper rivers come together to form the Atlantic Ocean. Captain George Cooper, one of General Francis Marion's men, took an active part in the Battle of Cypress Swamp (1781). Robert Muldrow Cooper (died 1966) served in the state House and Senate from Wisacky and for 44 years was trustee (with 15 years as chairman of the board) of Clemson University, where the R. M. Cooper Library is named for him. Two other libraries are named for Coopers: the Thomas Cooper Library on the Columbia campus of University of South Carolina is named for its past president and professor; and the John Hughes Cooper Branch Library in suburban Columbia's North Trenholm section is named for the attorney and large landowner in Forest Acres. Cooper House at Suttons along the Santee River in Williamsburg County was built in the early 1800s and is one of the oldest houses in the county. Simon Cooper Branch, between Sumter and Shaw Airforce Base on US 76, was called Green Swamp until 1890, when Simon Cooper was hanged there from a gum tree. County maps and records now mark the stream as Simon Cooper Branch. The Cooper name was also found early on in the upcountry. Before

1790 Charles Cooper was a landowner and resident of old Ninety Six (Cambridge) District.

Coosawhatchie
KOO-suh-HATCH-i (OO as in booze)

The unknowing sometimes put the w in the third syllable (KOO-sa-WAHTCH-i). It's an Indian word that may mean cane-creek people. Coosawhatchie is a little town in lowcountry Jasper County on US 278 and SC 462, off US 95, north of the county seat of Ridgeland.

Cordes
KOHRDZ (rhymes with boards)

But remember that the South Carolinian would almost make it two syllables, KOE-wuhdz. Named for the French Huguenot family who settled there, the town of Cordesville is on SC 402 in Berkeley County about ten miles southeast of the county seat, Moncks Corner. Josephine Cordes was postmistress of Ridgeville in Colleton County in 1867. And a hundred years later the name was found on the coast, Cordes Lucas being a resident of McClellanville.

Coronaca
KAHR-uh-NAE-kuh

It's the name of a town and creek in the upcountry on US 221, northeast of Greenwood. From earliest colonial times the name has been variously spelled: Cornacre in William Henry Drayton's *Memoirs*; Coronacre in Banastre Tarleton's *Campaigns*; Coronacay in the Indian books; and Corn-acre as the name of the landholdings of the gallant Jewish patriot of the Revolution, Francis Salvadore (1747?–1776). For Coronaca Creek, the early meaning "corn acres" refers to the level bottom land along its banks from its juncture upstream with Wilson Creek down to US 221.

Cote Bas
KOTE BAH

Before the French Huguenots gave the creek this spelling—French for low shores—the possibly Indian name had been variously spelled Coatbaw, Cutbaw, and Cortbaw. Cote Bas Creek flows into Back River near its junction with the Cooper River north of Charleston. As well as being a creek name, it was also a plantation on the neck of land at the junction of Back and Cooper rivers. Poet-novelist Drayton Mayrant remembers that as a child at the turn of the century she and her family took a trip up the river. As they rounded the neck at Cote Bas, they were loudly serenaded by the bleating of a flock of goats. Ever after, her family's name for the plantation was appropriately Goat Baa.

Courtenay
KOHRT-ni

Courtenay was a flagstop on the Southern Railway in Oconee County (northwestern corner of the state). It was named for William A. Courtenay (1831–1908), mill owner and former mayor of Charleston. He built his home, Innisfallen (for his ancestral Ireland), near Newry, a few miles northwest of Clemson University.

Couturier
kuh-TREH-uh

South Carolinians make three syllables of the four-syllable French. It was a Huguenot surname, and is preserved now among descendants as a first or middle name. Couturier Street in Eutawville (near Lake Marion in Orangeburg County) is named for the plantation owner who resided there. Couturier Lake in Berkeley County is also named for the early settlers. Descendants who bear the name include Harriet Couturier Thomas Ulmer of Columbia, Couturier Stedman of Charleston, and Harriet Couturier Gaillard of Eutawville.

Cowpens
KOW-PENZ

The folks in the little town haven't gotten above their raisings in their pronunciation of their town name, though newcomers to the state sometimes say KOW-penz or even KUP-penz. The town of Cowpens is now on US 29, off I 85, some ten miles northeast of Spartanburg. In Colonial times Hannah's Cowpens (some say Saunder's Cowpens) was the stopover for cattle drives from the upcountry; it was also a trading area with the Cherokee Indians. The Battle of Cowpens (January 17, 1781) was the first in an important series of decisive battles leading to the British defeat at Yorktown. There were 150 Revolutionary battles in South Carolina —more than in any other colony. Of the six important battles for which the Continental Congress authorized gold medals, two were in South Carolina: Cowpens and Eutaw Springs.

Cuffee
KUF-fi

The word is variously spelled Cuffe, Cuffy, and Cuffee. In old Edgefield District down toward the Savannah River there was a church 1764–1770 at Cuffe-Town in an area called Londonderry. Just before the Revolution a missionary recorded that there were 200 families there without the ordinances of religion "so that their children were growing up like savages." Cuffy Town Creek in the upcountry Greenwood and McCormick counties area runs through Cuffy Town, a settlement of Negroes sometimes called cuffies. The term cuffy to refer to a Negro child was also used in upper Richland County at the turn of the century.

Cumalander
KUM-uh-LAND-uh

This Dutch Fork name is sometimes spelled Comalander or Kumalander.

Currell
KUH-ruhl

Not too long ago a radio newsman reported a political meeting held at kuh-REL Building on the Columbia campus of the University of South Carolina. Immediately thereafter the station was deluged with telephone calls from former students of the colorful English professor and university president Dr. W. S. Currell, for whom the building is named. Fifty years later they still cared that his name be pronounced correctly. The red-brick building just behind the Observatory was originally the law school, and was called Petigru. Shakespeare was very real to Doctor Currell. On a hot August noon-day on Columbia's Main Street he stopped young Professor J. Milton Ariail to discuss at length whether Hamlet's mother Queen Gertrude had been in on the plot to kill Hamlet's father. Finally becoming exasperated with Professor Ariail's tendency to defend all women, Doctor Currell stomped his foot as he damned the queen, "Guilty as hell!" and stormed away from the gathered crowd. Cook's Map of 1766 has a marginal note that a Currell family was one of 26 families on Hilton Head Island at that time. Currell's Sink on that island was a natural depression in the shoreline along Scull Creek. Thomas Currell was living there in 1820.

Cuttino
KUT-in-NOE

The unknowing sometimes pronounce Cuttino as a Spanish name, kuh-TEE-NOE. This French Huguenot name, now spelled phonetically, was originally spelled Cothonneau. The family settled first in Charleston, then in Georgetown County, and now lives in Sumter. Charles L. Cuttino, Jr., of Sumter is a civil and family court judge. Dr. Mary Cuttino Crow Anderson, associate professor of English in the University of South Carolina General Studies Program, wrote her Ph.D. dissertation on South Carolina French Huguenots in fiction. Doctor Anderson makes the interesting observation that the French who moved inland early on usually kept the French pronunciations but adopted phonetic spellings of their names, whereas those who stayed on the coast usually kept the French spelling but Carolinized the pronunciation: Cuttino and DuPre are contrasting examples.

Dacus
DAE-kus

The upcountry Dacusville post office on SC 186 northeast of Pickens was named for the storekeeper and other Dacus families in the area. In a 1981 Spring Art Show, Furman University Professor Thomas E. Flowers won the top $2,000 prize for his oil landscape "Dacusville"—with the only drawback being the newscaster's calling it DAK-us-vil. Dacus Library at Winthrop College in Rock Hill is named for Ida Jane Dacus (1875–1964), the state's pioneer professional librarian and Winthrop's first librarian (1902–1945).

Dalcho
DAL-koe

Frederick Dalcho (1770–1836), M.D., editor of the Charleston *Courier* and priest of St. Michael's Episcopal Church in Charleston, was author of the history of South Carolina Episcopal Church, 1820, updated by Bishop Albert Sidney Thomas, 1957.

Dalzell
DAL-ZEL

Dalzell is a town east of Columbia on US 521 between Sumter and Camden. The town was named by a Scottish engineer who was building the railroad there, for a church in Dalziel, Lanarkshire, Scotland. The South Carolina family name Dalziel commemorates a brave act of their forebear: A near kinsman of King Kenneth II was hanged by the Picts. The king offered a reward to anyone who would retrieve the corpse. Finally one said "Dalziell," which meant "I dare." He rescued the body, and his posterity adopted the name Dalziel and the motto "I dare."

Dargan
DAHR-gun

The family name Dargan is of Irish origin. Timothy Dargan, a Baptist minister, was founder of Ebenezer Baptist Church in old Darlington District, now in Florence County. His many descendants included Congressman George W. Dargan (1841–1898) and John Julius Dargan (1848–1925), lawyer, educator, state legislator, advocate of women's suffrage and peace. Clara Victoria Dargan (born 1840) was a poet and fiction writer from Fairfield District. Olive Tilford Dargan (died 1968), poet and playwright, was called by Thomas Nelson Page the first American poet of her day.

Daufuskie
daw-FUS-ki

Daufuskie Island, south of Hilton Head Island, on maps and records has been variously spelled D'awfoski, Dawfuski, Dewfoskey, etc. On several early maps Calibogue Sound (between Daufuskie and Hilton Head) is recorded as Dawfuski River and Daufuski Sound. The island is separated from the mainland by the New River and the Cooper River. It is one of the smallest voting precincts in the state, with 52 registered voters in 1980, when only one voted in the Republican presidential primary. The word Daufuskie may be Indian for fork, though the fact that blending of languages (Indian, English, and Gullah) sometimes occurs makes the latest suggested origin worth telling: Daufuskie is the first inhabited island north of the Savannah River; therefore it's the first key, or, as the Gullah would say, dau fus key—hence Daufuskie. Or is this as far-fetched as the reluctant-mule story for Pocotaligo?

Deas
DAEZ (one syllable)

One of the most widely known twentieth-century men of this
name was Charlestonian William Deas, the black chef whose
Deas's she-crab soup made Everett's Restaurant a must for visitors
and home folks alike. The name Deas is of Scottish origin. Its
presence in South Carolina dates from Colonial times, with several of the name serving in the state legislature. William Allen
Deas (1784–1864) was secretary to Thomas Pinckney, United
States Minister to England. In Camden in the 1830s Colonel
James H. Deas presided over the group that initiated the building
of Grace Episcopal Church. Anne Simons Deas wrote a history
of the Ball family (1909). In lowcountry Berkeley County the
swamp on the Deas family property is now called by the flowery
and corrupted name Daisy's Swamp.

Debidue
DEB-i-DUE

Debidue Island is in coastal Georgetown County just south of
Pawley's Island. Its name is probably a corruption of the family
name of an early French settler, Debordieu or DeBordieu; that
name survives in DeBordieu Colony Club in the area of the old
Arcadia Plantation. However, there is a questionable ex post facto
story regarding the origin of the name: during a terrible storm and
shipwreck, the French passengers who finally made it to the shore
of this island fell on their knees and gave thanks for being saved
by the mercy of God—de bon Dieu.

DeGraffenreid
duh-GRAF-en-REED

One of Chester County's largest pre-Civil War planters, Thomas
DeGraffenreid was descended from Christopher, Baron DeGraffenreid, one of the early Carolina landgraves. His property in west-

ern Chester County was referred to as the Baron's Estate. The plantation burial ground is nearby on Fish Dam Road.

Dehon
duh-HONE (second syllable rhymes with CONE)

Dehon School (1851–1861) in Greenville was a parochial school of Christ Episcopal Church, named for the Right Reverend Theodore Dehon, second Bishop of the Diocese of South Carolina (1812–1817) and active in the founding of the General Theological Seminary in New York.

Deierlein
DEH-uh-LINE

Of German origin by way of the State of Washington, the name dates its South Carolina connection from Fort Jackson and World War II. The Stephen H. Deierlein family now lives in Columbia.

DeKalb
duh-KAB

The street in Camden and the little town on US 601 north of Camden are both named for Major General Baron DeKalb. A native of Germany, he was a hero, mortally wounded, in the Revolutionary Battle of Camden. DeKalb accompanied LaFayette when he first landed in America at North Island, the eastern shore of Winyah Bay near Georgetown. There is also a DeKalb Street in Georgetown.

DeLasteyrie

duh-LAS-tri

The Last Tree Place is on Wadmalaw Island, Charleston County, one mile from Rockville on SC 700—land given by William Seabrook to his daughter Martha Washington Seabrook. Maybe the name of the area is from a large old tree, the last one before the water's edge. But family records indicate that this is folk etymology: Martha Washington Seabrook married Count Ferdinand DeLasteyrie, reputedly the nephew of LaFayette. DeLasteyrie Place, their home, ere long was pronounced The Last Tree Place. During the Civil War the land and buildings were destroyed or damaged by the invading Union Army. The Count sued the United States Government for damage to the property of a French citizen. We've found no evidence as to whether the Count collected.

Derieux

DEH-ri-OE

Sam Arthur Derieux's *Frank of Freedom Hill* is a collection of twelve outdoor stories. His "Trial in Tom Belcher's Store" was included in the *Literature and Life* high school textbooks of the 1930s. Sam's brother Jim Derieux was a prominent newspaperman in Columbia, Richmond, and elsewhere in the Southeast. The site of the Derieux family home, 532 Harden Street in Five Points of Columbia, is now the location of Finlay House, the Episcopal retirement home. Sam and Jim Derieux's niece, Lottie Derieux ("Dolly") Hamby, former tennis champion, is partner in one of the first and most successful Southern advertising firms owned by women: Bradley, Graham, and Hamby in Columbia.

DeSaussure, deSaussure

DES-suh-soe, DES-suh-SOHR

The pronunciation is obviously South Carolina, not French. The building on the north side of the Horseshoe on the Columbia campus of the University of South Carolina is named for Henry W. DeSaussure, one of the first trustees of the South Carolina College. He was a descendant of Henri and Magdle DeSaussure, who in 1730 owned a 312-acre plantation, now part of Shipyard Plantation, on Hilton Head Island. Another son, Daniel (1736–1798), born at Pocotaligo, was a member of the Provincial Congress and the state legislature, J. M. DeSaussure was a mayor of Camden (1847–1848). Gertrude DeSaussure was a Charleston portrait painter. The Reverend Henry DeSaussure Bull of Georgetown wrote the history of his church, Prince George, Winyah—one of the few Episcopal churches to have a non-Biblical or non-liturgical name.

Des Champs
duh SHAMPS

The French name still survives in the Midlands. Buster DesChamps was one of Columbia High's best football players back in the 1930s. Frank J. DesChamps of Bishopville in Lee County told us a delightful story of the little "shortchange" store over that way in the 1800s called Pinch 'Em Slyly.

DesPortes
DES-POHRTS

The inconsistency of South Carolinians' pronunciation of French names is evident when this one is compared with the preceding Des Champs. Fay Allen DesPortes (1890–1944), United States Minister to Bolivia, Guatemala, and Costa Rica, was a Fairfield County merchant, farmer, and member of the state House and Senate. The name DesPortes is still prominent in Columbia and Winnsboro (US 321 north of Columbia).

DeTreville
DET-tri-VIL

DeTreville Avenue runs south off Forest Drive in northeast Columbia and Forest Acres. Richard DeTreville (1801–1874) represented Beaufort County in the state House and Senate, was lieutenant governor, and served in both the Mexican War and the Civil War. Marie L. DeTreville, retired teacher, now lives in Walterboro, and the late Julian DeTreville was a friend of the editors at Columbia's old Shandon School in the 1930s.

Devereaux
DEV-uh-ROE

Devereaux Street in the Heathwood section of eastern Columbia is named for the French Huguenot family. The name is also spelled without the *a*, Devereux. The plantation name in Natchez, Mississippi, is spelled D'Evereux. J. H. Devereaux was architect for Charleston's St. Matthew's Lutheran Church; the building was completed in 1872, and it burned in 1965. Mrs. Catherine Ann Devereux Edmondston's diary (1860–1866), published in 1980, includes poignant observations by a supporter of secession and extensive genealogical notes on the Devereux family.

Docheno
DOE-chuh-NOE

Docheno was a flagstop of the Southern Railway between Columbia and Greenville, a few miles southeast of Greenville. Though the origin of the name is unknown, there is an apocryphal story that it is folk etymology from "Don't you know?" The more likely explanation is that it is a corruption of the French Deux Cheneaux (Two Young Oak Trees), for the name of an inn or tavern there.

Doko
DOE-KOE

Since 1877 the town on US 21 between Columbia and Ridgeway has been called Blythewood. Prior to that it was called Doko, so named when the railroad was built from Columbia to Charlotte, North Carolina. Some think Doko is an Indian word referring to the train engine and meaning Iron Horse's watering place. It was from the town of Doko that General Wade Hampton on 18 February 1865 wired General P. G. T. Beauregard in Ridgeway requesting in vain permission to attack General William Tecumseh Sherman's divided corps one unit at a time. If such permission had been granted, Doko might have been famous as a battleground, as well as the birthplace of J. Gordon Coogler, Bard of the Congaree.

Dolan
DOE-lun

Seemingly memorializing a devout resident, Matthew Dolan African Methodist Episcopal is the name recorded on the U.S. Coastal and Geodetic Map of Wampee Quadrangle—the result either of poor listening by surveyors or poor talking by residents giving the information. Contrary to federal officialdom and according to markings on the marble cornerstone of the church in Little River Neck of the Grand Strand in Horry County, it's not Matthew Dolan at all, but "Macedonia African Methodist Episcopal Church, 1957." A Greek tourist from Canada was intrigued by the cornerstone and inquired about the possible Greek settlement there in earlier times. Although many of our place names recall the settlers' homelands, even more of them—as does this one—come from the Bible.

Dominick
DOM-uh-NIK, DOM-uh-NEK

This German-origin family, with both pronunciations, dates from Colonial times in the Midlands' Dutch Fork and is still present both there and in the upcountry. Bob Dominick sent *Names in South Carolina* the story of Ghost Creek Road in his native Laurens County. Ethel Wannamaker Dominick of Lake Murray near Prosperity, cousin-in-law of the late South Carolina Congressman Frederick H. Dominick, is an avid record-keeper of the Wannamaker and Dominick families.

Dorchester
DOHR-CHES-tuh

The name Dorchester came with the Puritans from England via Massachusetts to Colonial Carolina in 1695. Upon arrival in Charleston, one of the Puritans recorded that "the city has more taverns than churches." Seeking a more nearly sober atmosphere, the New England emigrants in 1696 moved twenty miles up the Ashley River to begin their town and church at Dorchester, with old Fort Dorchester built some 50 years later. Dorchester is the setting of the opening of William Gilmore Simms's Revolutionary War novel, *The Partisan*. Many of the original buildings were destroyed by the earthquake of 1886. The area is now a state park. Dorchester County is west of Charleston and Berkeley counties, and the present town of Dorchester is on US 78 between Ridgeville and St. George.

Dorroh
DUH-ruh

It's a family name that was almost a town name. But the fact that there were more Methodists than Presbyterians in the voting precinct resulted in the town's being called Gray Court (SC 101 and SC 14, off US 276, in Laurens County). Robert Adams Gray, grandfather of renowned educator Dr. Wil Lou Gray, was the first extensive cotton planter in upcountry Laurens County. He gave land for the railroad and the depot and was active in community affairs and the Methodist Church. In the same area Miss Sallie Dorroh as early as 1883 managed the post office—unofficially called by her name—and was an active Presbyterian. By 1894 the community had grown sufficiently to warrant an official name. Which should it be—Gray for the benefactor or Dorroh for the revered postmistress? The election in February 1894 was a line-up of Methodist and Presbyterian voters, and Gray was the winner. A now unknown telegraph operator, wiring in the results, added Court "to give the name an English flavor." The Gray family has now spread near and far, but keeps posted via the historian of the clan, Marguerite Tolbert, granddaughter of Robert Adams Gray and retired head of state adult education.

Doty
DOE-ti

It's a prominent name in the Midlands, especially in Winnsboro, county seat of Fairfield County, north of Columbia. The family name is included here not so much because it is mispronounced as because, when heard, it is sometimes misspelled Doughty, another prominent Midlands name. Doughty, not related to uncooked bread, is pronounced DOW-ti, the first syllable rhyming with NOW.

Dougherty
DOW-uhr-ti (first syllable rhymes with NOW)

Bryant and John Dougherty were in Camden (one of the earliest towns in the Midlands) by 1780. Later and farther upcountry, the Rev. George Dougherty established the Dougherty Manual Labor School in 1837 at Cokesbury Community near Greenwood (off US 178 on SC 254).

Doughty
DOW-ti (first syllable rhymes with NOW)

Doughty Lake in Clarendon County is a long, narrow body of water on the edge of Santee River forest, a few miles below old Nelson's Ferry. The Nelson house (built 1762) was once the home of William Doughty, layreader of lower St. Mark's Church. Doughty Street in Charleston is in the Medical University section. (Doughty Street in London is famous as the home of Charles Dickens.) Benjamin R. Doughty was postmaster of Fair Play in upcountry Pickens County in 1867. Dr. Roger Doughty (1895–1950), descendant of Georgia medical school deans, was himself a prominent Columbia physician and consultant to the Veterans' Hospital.

Duane
DWANE, duh-WANE

Regarding the pronunciation, you'll have to ask the owner of this one, though as a surname it's more often the one-syllable DWANE, *e.g.*, Mrs. William Ravenel Duane of Bram's Point, Hilton Head Island.

Due West (DeWitt)
DUE WEST

Over two hundred years ago it was DeWitt's Corner, a trading post on the old Cherokee Path. In early records it was variously spelled DeWitt's, Dewises, Devises, or Duets. The 1777 treaty of South Carolina with the Cherokee Indians is recorded as the Treaty of Dewitt's Corner. From 1820 on, DeWitt and Due West are used interchangeably. (DeWitt was pronounced doo-Wet or doo-ET; oo as in boot). The town of Due West (SC 184, north of Abbeville) is not at a westward turn in the trail, nor it is due west of some other place or boundary; the name is a corruption or folk etymology of the original name. Today Due West is the seat of Erskine College, the oldest denominational college in the state, an Associate Reformed Presbyterian institution. Due West is called the A.R.P.'s Holy City. DeWitt's Corner Brook in Abbeville and Anderson counties is now called Corner Creek.

Dulin
DOO-lin (OO as in boot)

This family name, present in the Midlands, is too often pronounced DOE-lun—perhaps because it is confused with Dolan—and too often misspelled Dublin.

DuPre
duh-PREE

It's a lowcountry French Huguenot family that settled in the Santee River delta. Daniel Warren DuPre was a planter and minister of St. James, Santee. His home, called Echaw (EE-chaw), was moved piece by piece by his descendants down the various rivers and creeks to its present location at McClellanville. Though the family name is now spread about, members still return home for reunions at "The Village" (McClellanville, located on Jeremy Creek off US 17 on SC 45 between Charleston and Georgetown). Other branches of DuPres have now moved into the state, especially from North Carolina, and some pronounce the name doo-PRAE (oo as in boot) or spell it Dupree.

Dutch (Deutsch)
DUCH

Though it comes from the German word Deutsch meaning German, no South Carolinian would twist his mouth enough to say DOICH. The Dutch Fork area includes parts of Richland, Lexington, and Newberry counties. It is the area—the fork—between the Saluda and Broad rivers before they come together at Columbia to form the Congaree River. The fork was settled by Germans in the 1730s and 1740s. Though the name has nothing to do with the Netherlands, the big Dutch Square shopping mall in the area has a large Holland windmill at its entrance. And to confuse nationalities further, business booms when Dutch Square's anniversary sales—called Mardi Gras—are anachronistically held in August on Thursday, Friday, and Saturday. The name Dutch Fork has also been used in the area for a baseball league, post office branch, businesses, and several churches. In Charleston, Clifford Street, the location of St. John's Lutheran Church, was formerly called Dutch Church Alley.

Dyches
DIKES

Dyches family members, of German origin, are still residents of Barnwell County. Byron Dyches recently prepared an interesting article on the use of folk medicine in the area. Back in 1942 at York High School Nettie Lee Dyches was a crowd-pleasing basketball player. Dyches Mill was about twenty miles south of Barnwell near Beldock (Baldoc) in what is now Allendale County, bordering the Savannah River. The area was part of a large land grant to Dr. Elijah Gillett for his services in the Revolution. In Gillett's 1817 will Dyches Mill Plantation was left to his daughter Lavinia. On the Mills Atlas of 1824 it is recorded as Gillett's Mill.

Eaddy
EE-di

The double-d Eaddy name is of English origin and is now found over much of the state, especially in Winnsboro, Florence, Johnsonville, and Myrtle Beach. Eadytown, in the triangle of SC 45 and roads 31 and 23, is ten miles west of Pineville in lowcountry Berkeley County. It is named for the landowning black Eady family, who are still there. The story is told that soon after 1865 the town was named Lincolnville for the President who signed the Emancipation Proclamation, but it has now long been called Eadytown. Both spellings are pronounced Eady.

58

Eakin
AE-kin

Upcountry Eakin's Mill was a nineteenth-century grist mill on Job's Creek, just east of Gilgal Methodist Church in old Abbeville District. The identically pronounced Aiken family is also prominent in the area.

Eargle
UHR-gul

Of German origin, the Eargle family settled in the Dutch Fork in the 1740s and is still present in the Midlands. Herbert Eargle, who grew up on Wateree Creek, recalled the handed-down story of the origin of the nearby community of White Rock: it was the location of flint white rock, and Indians came from as far away as the Savannah River to secure it for making their arrowheads. The late D. Hoye Eargle was an honor student at the University of South Carolina in the 1930s and became a renowned geologist with the United States government in Texas.

Earle
UHRL, UHR-ul, UHL

The pronunciation of this name depends on how distinctly its owner chooses to pronounce the *r*. Earles Grove is a community, school, and church in the northwest county of Oconee. Earle's Bridge, across the Seneca River, is on the road from Anderson to Townville. An old Earle homestead, called Evergreen, was located along the Savannah River near the Anderson County line. Earleville, in upcountry Spartanburg County, was settled before the Revolution by brothers John and Bayles Earle from Virginia. Earle's Ford (now named Landrum in Spartanburg County for Baptist preacher John Gill Landrum) was the site of a Revolutionary battle. Earlewood Park in north Columbia is named for F. S. Earle, two-term mayor of the city. The oldest house in

Greenville, 107 James Street (now the home of historian Mary C. Simms Oliphant), was built in 1810, home of Elias T. Earle. Colonel Earle was state senator, U.S. Congressman, silk grower, manufacturer, and Commissioner of Indian Affairs. Colonel Earle is reputed to have given the name Dark Corner to the upper Greenville section: a tax appraiser went to a humble log cabin up in the hills. The man of the house wasn't at home, and his wife came to the door with a shot gun.

"What you want?"
"Congress wants to know what your husband's land's worth."
"My ole man'll go up there and whup Mr. Congress for come meddlin' in our 'fairs."

As she raised the shotgun, the tax appraiser made a hasty retreat down the hill. When Colonel Earle heard the story, he chuckled, "That must be the dark corner of the district." And it's been called Dark Corner ever since. At least that's one of the stories of its origin. But it was also at Dark Corner that one of the finest early schools flourished—Moffattsville. And it was the Rev. S. J. Earle of Dark Corner who operated Gowanville Academy, established 1880. From 1798 to 1916, the counties of Spartanburg, Greenville, Sumter, and Oconee together had one or more Senator Earles in the state legislature. The name still has many representatives, including Samuel Broadus Earle, Jr., an Anderson architect, and Julius Richard Earle, a Walhalla physician.

Eastover
EEST-OE-vuh

The lower Richland town of Eastover on SC 764, south of US 76, may be so named because it is east over from Columbia.

Ebaugh
EE-BOE

The family of this name came to South Carolina from Maryland. *Little David*, the small torpedo-like semi-submarine which in 1864 attacked and seriously damaged the Federal warship *New Iron-sides* in Charleston Harbor, was built by and named for David Chenoweth Ebaugh. His granddaughter Laura Smith Ebaugh is a professor of sociology at Furman University in Greenville. Donald Ebaugh was organist at St. John's Episcopal Church, Shandon, in Columbia in the 1930s.

Edisto
ED-is-TOE

Edisto Island, Edisto River, Edisto Gardens at Orangeburg—the name is so much a part of nearly everyday speech that we almost didn't include it among the difficults. But then we learned that researchers at the University of South Carolina's Caroliniana Library often ask for information about "the ed-IS-toe Indians," and just recently a radio newscaster spoke of the Indian community of Four Hole in the Colleton and Dorchester counties area as having once been a part of "the ed-IS-toe tribe." Though Indians didn't record their languages, so that spellings may vary in records depending on what the recorder heard, usage determines the pronunciation; since Edisto has been ED-is-TOE in South Carolina for over 300 years, that's as it should be, e-DIS-toe researchers and newscasters to the contrary.

Ehrhardt
EHR-HAHRT

The town, at US 601 and SC 64, south of Bamberg and Little Salkehatchie River, is named for a German settler. Since the 1976 Bicentennial, Ehrhardt has sponsored the Schutzenfest (shooting festival) each August. The Ehrhardt family name is now found throughout the state, especially in Orangeburg, Columbia, and Charleston.

61

Ehrlich
UHR-LIK

The Ehrlich family, of German origin, is found throughout the
state, with notably different branches in Columbia and Chester.
The name means honorable. Michael Ehrlich came to Columbia
in 1840.

Eleazer
EL-i-AZE-uh

Johannes Stephen Eleazer from Germany settled in 1751 in the
middle of the Dutch Fork at Spring Hill. The ancestral home is
still there. J. H. Eleazer, a descendant of Johannes and later of
Clemson, wrote a widely read column for newspapers for over
50 years while serving as Saluda County Agricultural Agent. His
popular book *Dutch Fork Farm Boy* was published by the University of South Carolina Press in 1952. The family name Eleazer
is still prominent in the Midlands of South Carolina.

Elgin
EL-jin, EL-gin

Formerly Blaney, the town of Elgin (on US 1 northeast of Columbia) in Kershaw County was named for the Elgin Watch Company, which has now closed its operation there and left the town
only its name, pronounced EL-jin. The identically named community in Lancaster County near the North Carolina line most
likely got its name from Elgin District of Scotland, since the Lancaster community is near the Waxhaws (the area east of the
Wateree River and near the North Carolina line), known in our
early history as "the Scots' backdoor to South Carolina." Their
Scottish pronunciation was with the hard g, EL-gin, but the
townspeople now pronounce the name with the j sound, EL-jin.

Ellerbe

EL-uh-bi

The town of Ellerbe in Sumter County (east of Columbia) is named for the family of Thomas Ellerbe, who came to South Carolina in 1740. He was one of the first slaveowners on the upper Peedee River. Among the family's public servants have been senators from Chesterfield, Marlboro, and Marion counties; Governor William Haselden Ellerbe, who served 1897–1899; and Clarence McCall Ellerbe, soil scientist of Columbia. Among recent Ellerbe teachers have been three at Columbia High School: Eva Ellerbe, Latin teacher; Isla Ellerbe, English teacher; and Sarah Ellerbe Godbold, physical education teacher.

Elloree

EL-oh-REE

Elloree may be an Indian word meaning "home I love." The town at the intersection of SC 6 and SC 47 in Orangeburg County was named Popular Post Office by William J. Snyder, Baptist preacher and merchant there in 1837. Some time after that his wife renamed it Elloree—its present, official name.

Enoree

EN-oh-REE

Consistent with the abundance of wild grapes in this upcountry area, the river and town of Enoree in Spartanburg County have an Indian name reputed to mean "river of muscadines." The town was first called Mountain Shoals in the 1830s. Often traces for the horses were made from the grapevines that were so prolific along the banks of the Enoree River. Seth Poole bought land there in the 1830s, and much of that land bordering the Enoree River in Laurens County is still in the Poole family.

Erskine

UHR-skin

Erskine College of Due West (SC 20 and SC 184) in upcountry
Abbeville County was named for the Reverends Ebenezer and
Ralph Erskine, who founded the Associate (Secession) Church
of Scotland—now called Associate Reformed Presbyterian Church.
Begun as Mount Vernon Academy in 1836, then chartered as
Clark and Erskine Seminary in 1837 (Reverend Thomas Clark,
"father of the ARP Church in the South," came to the Long Cane
section of Abbeville in 1784), Erskine College was the first four-
year denominational school in South Carolina. Erskine Street in
eastern Columbia is one of several streets in the Jackson Heights
residential area named for South Carolina colleges.

Estill

ES-tul

The town of Estill (US 321 and SC 3) is in Hampton County,
which borders the Savannah River. It was officially named in 1905
for Colonel James Holbrook Estill, once owner of the Savannah
Morning News. It is frequently mispronounced with the second
syllable accented, es-STIL and es-STEL.

Eutawville

yoo-TAW-vul, yoo-TAW-VIL (OO as in hoot)

The Indian word Eutaw may mean sand or pine. Residents of the
town and area are more apt to use the first pronunciation, yoo-
TAW-vul, with yoo-TAW-VIL more often used by folks from
other parts of the state. The town of Eutawville (SC 6 and SC
453) in Orangeburg County was chartered by the legislature
in 1888. Early plantations had been established around Eutaw
Springs on grants dating from 1703. The area grew as a summer
village for those who wished to escape lowland mosquitoes. On
September 8, 1781, "at Eutaw Springs the valiant died" in the last

important battle of the Revolution in South Carolina. The Springs, at the time of the battle, was owned by James McKelvey or his heirs. In 1849 William Sinkler owned Eutaw Plantation. Much of the area was flooded by the Santee-Cooper hydroelectric project, which formed Lake Marion, but the battle site, which was on high land, was spared.

Evans

IV-inz, EV-unz

You'll have to ask, since each pronunciation is required by one branch of Evanses or another, but there are differences of opinion even in the same family. Most of them today use the short e sound, EV-unz. John Gary Evans (governor from 1894 to 1897), gave to the town of Edgefield (US 25 and SC 23) a 40-acre estate as a Red Shirt Shrine in memory of his uncle General Martin Witherspoon Gary, who began the movement to redeem the state from Carpetbag rule during Reconstruction. Between 1814 and 1918 seven Evans men served in the state Senate from five different counties: Aiken, Chesterfield, Fairfield, Marion, and three from Marlboro. Alexander Evins served as senator from Pendleton District from 1842 to 1854; he was one of the first physicians in the new upcountry town of Anderson (founded in 1828). On the 1820 Robert Mills map Evan's Mill is located near Lebanon Church about six miles southeast of Abbeville. Other maps of the period place Evans Ferry near Johns Creek Road about five miles from Bennettsville (in Marlboro County) on the road to Blenheim. Evans Motor Company at the corner of Gervais and Harden streets in mid-twentieth-century Columbia was one of the busiest service stations in town. The name was then pronounced IV-inz. Walker, Evans, and Cogswell is a long-time printing firm in Charleston; the name is pronounced EV-unz.

Faust

FAWST (rhymes with exhaust)

Faust families of German origin settled in the Dutch Fork area. Contrary to the pronunciation of Marlowe's *Doctor Faustus*, with

au as ow in now, members of the family in the Midlands pronounce the au as aw in raw. Jacob Faust had land grants in 1763
on a branch of Crane Creek in upper Richland County. John,
Daniel, and Gaspar were also pre-Revolutionary Fausts in the
area. The 1790 census spells the name Foost. Faust Department
Store was long a business on Columbia's Assembly Street.

Fenwick
FEN-ik

Fenwick Hall, the 1730 Georgian mansion on John's Island, has
recently been restored, and in 1980 it was opened as a private
alcoholic treatment facility. The lowcountry Fenwick family of
English origin came to Charleston about 1700 from Barbados.
Fenwick Island, in Colleton County, lies in the neck between the
Ashepoo and the South Edisto rivers. John Fenwick owned land
on Hilton Head Island in 1783. In the Revolutionary battle at
Mathew's Plantation (May 20, 1779) on the Stono River on John's
Island, the patriots were surprised through the treachery of a
local loyalist, Thomas Fenwick, and were shown no quarter.

Fouche
foo-SHAE (oo as in booze)

The French family name has variant spellings. James and Heyward Fouche are Columbia physicians. The 1790 census lists
Charles Foushee in Orangeburg District. On Mills Atlas (1820)
there is a Forshe homesite near Cambridge in old Abbeville District (now Greenwood County). Charles Fooshe, deacon in Siloam
Baptist Church (now Sylom Meeting House), is listed as Fooche
on church records.

Fowble
FOW-buhl (ow as in now)

Deane G. Fowble, father and son, were University of South Carolina football players and now live in the Columbia area. Contrary to the way reminiscing sportscasters would have it, their name is not pronounced FOE-bul.

Gadsden
GADZ-dun

Christopher Gadsden (1724–1805) was a Charleston merchant, served in the Commons House of Assembly, was a delegate to the First Continental Congress and a brigadier-general in the Continental Army. Named for landowners in lower Richland County, the little town of Gadsden is southeast of Columbia on SC 48 and SC 769. Thomas Cain was postmaster of Gadsden in 1867 when there were only two other post offices in the county (Columbia and Hopkins' Turnout). Charleston County had only four, in contrast to Pickens and Anderson districts in the upcountry with seventeen and thirteen respectively. Lack of roads and difficulty of travel probably accounted for more post offices in the hilly upcountry.

Gaillard
gil-YAHD

A lake, street, road, auditorium, and island in the state are named for this prominent French Huguenot family. And the unknowing still call it GAE-LAHRD. The Gaillard family first came to South Carolina in 1685 with land warrants for 600 acres—land still in the family and farmed today by Mr. and Mrs. Richard B. (Harriet Clarkson) Gaillard of Eutawville. Gaillard Street in that town is named for Joachim Gaillard, an early plantation owner. Colonel David DuBose Gaillard (1859–1913), engineer, was in charge of excavating and dredging the Panama Canal. Gaillard Cut in

Panama is named for him. His grandfather, David St. Pierre Gaillard, lived at Spring Vale Plantation (sixteen miles north of Winnsboro in the Midlands) and raised his seven sons and six daughters there. Several Gaillards served in the state Senate. Palmer Gaillard is former mayor of Charleston. Samuel E. Gaillard (born about 1840) was a black Republican state senator during Reconstruction who migrated to Liberia in 1878. Gilliard is possibly a phonetic spelling of the same name, taken by black families. Melvin R. Gilliard of Yonges Island retired in 1980 after 34 years with the state highway department. Similarly, Gillard Town in Berkeley County is a black community one and a half miles from SC 311 and SC 27, named for the resident Gillard family, pronounced gil-AHRD.

Gallivant
GAL-li-vunt

The town of Gallivant's Ferry in northwest Horry County is on the Little Peedee River at US 501. The name of the first ferryman (dating from 1792) is variously spelled in records as Richard Gallevan, Gallivant, and Galliwan. J. W. Holliday came to the state from Virginia in 1869 and in the section of Gallivant's Ferry reputedly raised the first tobacco in South Carolina. The politically active Holliday family began having the now famous Gallivant's Ferry stump meeting in 1880. It's still the first every election year, with chicken bog the main course for the hungry candidates and their even hungrier following.

Gascoigne
GAS-koe-ni

In 1729 Captain John Gascoigne was owner of the 500-acre Fairfield Plantation on Hilton Head Island. Gaskin Bank (pronounced GAS-kin), extending about fifteen miles out into the Atlantic Ocean from Hilton Head Island, was apparently named for John Gascoigne, but simplified in spelling and pronunciation.

Gaud
GOWD (rhymes with loud)

Porter-Gaud, an Episcopal Church-related school in Charleston, was established in 1867 as Porter Military Academy. The Rev. A. Toomer Porter founded the school as a memorial to his young son, who had died of yellow fever. In 1965 the academy combined with Gaud School and moved to its present location at Albemarle Point.

Geechee
GEE-chi (hard G)

A Geechee is a tidewater South Carolinian whose speech is "different"—some say influenced by Gullah—in the pronunciation of such words as shrimp, milk, house, Charleston, boat. In fact, it's almost another language, called Charlestonese by writer Frank Gilbreth (alias Lord Ashley Cooper) in his *News and Courier* column, "Doing the Charleston." "Are you geechee?" also means "Are you ticklish?"

Geiger
GEE-guh (hard G's)

The Geiger Counter for detection of radioactivity is properly pronounced GIE-guh, but not so for the Dutch Fork Geiger family, now widespread in the Midlands. Early Geiger landowners were Jacob Geiger opposite Saxe Gotha in 1748 and John Jacob Geiger in upper Richland District near Cedar Creek in 1743. Not as immortalized through poetry as Paul Revere, but just as important to the patriots' cause, Emily Geiger also made a daring ride during the Revolution to deliver a message regarding British activity. A plaque in the State House lobby commends her for her bravery.

Gervais
juhr-VAE

Running east and west in front of the State House, Gervais Street in Columbia is named for John Lewis Gervais (1742–1798). He came to America in 1764 from France or Germany. A colonel in the Revolution, he was later a member of the Continental Congress and represented Ninety Six and Abbeville districts in the state Senate. It was Gervais who in 1786 introduced the bill naming the new state capital Columbia—a name to be frequently imitated in the umpteen Columbias and Columbuses throughout this nation.

Gibert
ji-BUHRT

Jean Louis Gibert was pastor and leader of the French Huguenot settlement of New Bordeaux (1764) in old Abbeville District. Anne Gibert, a genealogist who now lives in Columbia, has written a history of the upcountry Huguenot settlement and her forebears, *The Devoted Huguenot* (1976). Presently called Bordeaux, the town (between US 378 and SC 81) is in McCormick County near Clark Hill Reservoir.

Gignilliat
JIN-LAT, JIN-i-LAT

This one stumped even some fifth-generation natives, who gave it hard G's and sounded four-syllables, gig-NIL-li-AT, until an excellent historian of many South Carolina families, the late Mac Stubbs (Thomas M. Stubbs), told them better. And you have to listen closely to hear the occasionally pronounced middle syllable. In 1732 Henry Gignilliat owned 50 acres of land on Congaree River. The French Huguenot family name is still present today in several parts of the state. Charles Gignilliat of Spartanburg, through the South Carolina Historical Society, has recently established a college scholarship for descendants of French Huguenots. Julian H. Gignilliat is a Columbia attorney.

Gilchrist

GIL-krist

Gilchrist Bridge was named for the landowner Dr. David Gilchrist. In 1838 Doctor Gilchrist bought all John Newsom's land on the Little Peedee River. The bridge was located where Old Stage Road crossed the river, 100 feet north of the present US 76 bridge, east of Mullins in Marion County.

Gillespie

gil-LES-pi

Gillespie Mill Pond in Marlboro County of the Peedee section was named for the early Scot settler who brought the first boat to Cheraw (US 1 and SC 9) in 1743. Dizzy Gillespie, nationally renowned black jazz horn player, is a native of Cheraw. Three Gillespie brothers—James, Francis, and Samuel—were members of General Thomas Sumter's company of volunteers (1780) and are credited with naming Sumter The Gamecock. The Gillespies, much into cock fighting, had a famous blue hen and a cock named Tuck, which would fight successfully anywhere anytime—just like the General, whom they affectionately called "one of the blue hen's chickens." Hence came about the General's sobriquet, "The Gamecock." The family name Gillespie is now present throughout the state. There is also a Gillespie County in Texas—one of seventeen Texas counties named for South Carolinians who went to Texas and made outstanding contributions to its early history.

Girardeau

JUHR-ruh-DOE

Girardeau Avenue in Columbia and Forest Acres is named for the French Huguenot family. Although many of the Charleston Huguenots became Anglicans, elsewhere others became Presbyterians. For example, in tidewater McClellanville after the Civil War the Presbyterians gave up their country church (Old Wappetaw, some twenty miles from town) and built a handsome New Wappetaw Presbyterian Church in town. The dedicating minister was the Rev. John Girardeau.

Gist

GIST (hard G)

Though the common noun meaning the main point of the matter, gist, follows the pronunciation rule that g followed by i has a j sound, the family name still present in South Carolina and Gist Street in Columbia are properly pronounced with the hard g. Like other streets running north and south in the original plan for Columbia (1786), Gist Street is named for a Revolutionary general, Mordecai Gist of Maryland, who served in South Carolina in the latter part of the war. Two expressions refer to more recent structures on Columbia's general-named streets. "He now lives on Gist Street" used to be a euphemistic way of saying he's serving time in Central Correctional Institution, located on Gist Street before it was expanded to absorb the street. "He oughta be on Bull Street" means he's off his rocker, since the state mental hospital is located there. Two other prominent South Carolinians of the past were Gists. The young Confederate brigadier, General States Rights Gist (1831–1864), was killed at the Battle of Franklin, Tennessee. (States Rights is still a given name in the Gist family.) William Henry Gist was governor during the Civil War. His two-story brick home (built 1828) and rose garden in Union (US 176 and SC 49) were purchased by the state in 1960 and are maintained by the state park and forestry departments. Our late Columbia friend "Miss Lizz" (Mrs. W. Bedford Moore), patron of the arts and of *Names in South Carolina*, was a Gist descendant.

Gluck
GLOOK (oo as in boot; rhymes with Luke)

Gluck Mill is an upcountry textile mill near the town of Anderson (US 76 and SC 81). It's apparently a family name of German origin.

Gonzales
gon-ZA-LEEZ (on as in continent)

When *The State* newspaper publisher Ambrose Gonzales Hampton died in 1980, television newscasters marred the lengthy obituaries by displaying their Spanish knowledge and pronouncing his middle name gon-ZAH-lis. *The State* sponsors the University of South Carolina Gonzales Award, which some unknowing professor at the annual April Awards Day Ceremony almost regularly presents as the gon-ZAH-lis Award. Spanish to the contrary, this family pronounces the name gon-ZA-LEEZ. But Representative James E. Gonzales, North Charleston Republican, pronounces his name gon-ZAH-lis. The Cuban insurgent and refugee "General" Ambrosio José Gonzales became a United States citizen in 1849 and served in the Confederate army as a colonel. His sons Ambrose E. and N. G. were founders of Columbia's *The State* newspaper (1891). Ambrose E. Gonzales wrote *The Black Border* (1922), the famous collection of Gullah dialect stories, and was a forebear of the Hampton family, still associated with the newspaper. In the Tillman-Gonzales pen-and-gun slinging political feud (1903), editor N. G. Gonzales was killed, and his adversary, James H. Tillman (nephew of Governor and U.S. Senator Benjamin Ryan Tillman), was acquitted.

Goshen
GO-shun (rhymes with notion)

The name Goshen is of Biblical origin, meaning good farm land. Goshen Township in upcountry Union County contrasted appropriately with nearby Pea Ridge, reputedly so named because the ridge land "was too poor to sprout peas." Goshen Plantation in lowcountry Clarendon County was along the Santee River near Nelson's Ferry. The house dates back to 1762 in the Colonel Samuel Warren Nelson family, forebears of the Patrick Henry Nelson family of Stateburg and Columbia. Goshen Plantation in Calhoun County near the Congaree and Santee rivers became part of Lang Syne Plantation, owned by Langdon Cheves and later by the Peterkin family. There Pulitzer Prize Winner Julia Mood Peterkin (author of *Scarlet Sister Mary*) wrote her novels.

Goucher

GOW-chuh (GOW rhymes with NOW)

The area around Goucher Creek and Thicketty Fort was the scene of much Revolutionary fighting. Thicketty Fort (Fort Anderson) was built for the colonists' protection from the Cherokee Indians a quarter-mile from Goucher Creek in a thickly wooded section of what is now southwestern Cherokee County (one of the northwest counties bordering North Carolina); it became a loyalist stronghold until South Carolina partisans took the garrison without firing a shot in July 1780.

Goudelock

GOWD-LOK

Marine Lt. Bill Goudelock, son of the Felix Goudelocks and former student body president of Columbia High School, was killed in the third week of the Korean War. Memorial Stadium was dedicated to Bill and the other war casualties from Columbia area schools.

Gourdin
guh-DINE (hard g)

The Williamsburg County town of Gourdin (SC 375 and SC 377) on the Santee River was settled prior to 1744 and named for the Peter Gourdin family, early French Huguenots in the area. Gourdin's Depot was named for Captain Theodore Gourdin, who gave the land for the Northwestern Railroad to pass through this Santee area. The train was called Swamp Rabbit because of its many stops and starts. Virginia Gourdin, representing Charleston County, was one of the first women to be elected to the state legislature. The name is also spelled with an e (Gourdine) by some black families and pronounced guh-DEEN.

Gressette
GRES-et

Only a very new newcomer occasionally calls this one gruh-SET. Lawrence Marion Gressette (born 1902) of St. Matthews, Calhoun County (south of Columbia), has served since 1936 in the state Senate, of which he is president pro tem. His wisdom and grey hair are acknowledged in his sobriquet, The Grey Fox. Because so many bills never make it back to the Senate floor from the Judiciary Committee which he heads, that committee is called Gressette's Graveyard. The new Senate office building behind the State House in Columbia has been named for him. Following the Southern custom of consanguinity, we call him Cousin Marion since his paternal first cousin married our paternal uncle, Dr. Jean Baptiste LaBorde.

Grimball
GRIM-buhl

Paul Grimball, secretary of the Lords Proprietors, settled with his wife and daughter on a 600-acre grant on the North Edisto River in the 1680s. The remains of a tabby structure, said to be the original Grimball home, still stand at Point of Pines Plantation. (Tabby is a construction material of crushed oyster shells and lime.) Circuit Judge John Grimball and John B. Grimball, Columbia attorney, are among the descendants of Paul Grimball.

Grimké
GRIM-ki

Thomas Smith Grimké (1786–1834), philanthropist, educator, and reformer, represented the parishes of St. Philip and St. Michael in the state Senate, 1826–1830. The most famous of the Grimké name, Sarah (1792–1873) and Angelina (1805–1879), were daughters of Judge J. F. Grimké in Charleston. They were religiously devoted to Quakerism and to their antislavery convictions, so Sarah moved to Philadelphia in 1821 and Angelina followed in 1829. Beginning in 1835, they became active abolitionists and leaders in the women's suffrage movement. Grimkeville (old Rocky Mount) is located on the Catawba River in the upper Midlands near Great Falls.

Gulco
GUL-KOE

Gulco was the plantation of E. J. Gulledge and his first wife Lucy Coulter Gulledge in the Wedgefield community (SC 261) of Sumter County. The concocted name Gulco combines the first letters of the husband-wife family names.

Guerard
guh-RAHD

This prominent family is of French Huguenot origin. Réné Petit and Jacob Guérard petitioned the English Crown for permission to transport on a naval vessel several Protestant families to South Carolina to undertake the production of silk, oil, and wine. The first contingent of the Petit-Guérard Colony landed at Oyster Point, Charleston, in April 1680. From St. Helena in the Beaufort area, Benjamin Guerard (about 1733–1788) served in the Revolution, the Commons House of Assembly, the state House and Senate, and as Governor (1783–1785). The late Martha Guerard of Columbia was a professional genealogist, specializing in French Huguenot research.

Guerry
GEHR-ri (rhymes with berry)

Guerry Lake is a swamp lake located at or near the mouth of Savannah Creek, about four miles northwest of Jamestown in lowcountry Berkeley County's Hell Hole Swamp. William Alexander Guerry was bishop of the Episcopal Diocese of South Carolina, 1908–1928. His son Edward Brailsford Guerry was also an Episcopal clergyman, having been first a practicing attorney at law. Dr. LeGrand Guerry of Columbia was a renowned surgeon in the mid-twentieth century.

Guignard
gin-YAHD (hard g)

Mispronouncing a place name wouldn't necessarily cost a candidate an election, but it didn't help when the candidate's new office manager from out-of-state kept telling callers that the Lexington stump meeting was to be held in JIN-yud Park. Guignard Park in Cayce (just west of Columbia across the Congaree River) is named for the French Huguenot family that owned vast properties there and, until 1979, operated Guignard Brickworks, the longest continuously running family brickyard in the United States. Still Hopes, the Episcopal retirement home, is named for the old Guignard plantation, on which it stands. The Horry-Guignard House (corner of Senate and Pickens streets in Columbia) was the home of Colonel Peter Horry, Revolutionary patriot, and his wife, Margaret Guignard, daughter of Gabriel Guignard, founder of this family in South Carolina. John Gabriel Guignard

(1751–1822), Surveyor General of the state, also lived in this house. His family still has the compass he used to lay out the town of Columbia. (The family of Philip Pearson has his compass and claims that he was the town surveyor.) Guignard Drive in Sumter is named for Guignard Richardson (died 1880), a large landowner and resident of the area. The Ginyard family in Aiken and Columbia may have a phonetic spelling of the same name.

Guilds
GILEZ (one syllable, hard G, long I)

Dr. John C. Guilds, Methodist minister, was president of Columbia College. His son, John C. Guilds, Jr., has served on the faculty and administration of universities in Texas, South Carolina, and Arkansas.

Guillebeau
GIL-i-BOE

The French Huguenot family of André Guillebeau settled in upcountry Abbeville District in the vicinity of New Bordeaux (now in McCormick County). The family home and cemetery are located on SC 81.

Haltiwanger
HAWL-ti-WAHNG-uh

A goodly number of illustrious citizens of Lexington, Richland, and Orangeburg counties have borne this Swiss-German name. You pronounce it to rhyme with longer, not banger.

Hanahan
HAN-uh-HAN

The town of Hanahan in Berkeley County, north of Charleston, off I 26 and US 52, perpetuates the name of J. Ross Hanahan. He was the Charleston businessman who donated the land for the site of the Charleston waterworks. Hanahan on Edisto Island, between Charleston and St. Helena Sound, is named for a former landowner. The native blacks call Hanahan HIN-yunz.

Happoldt
hap-POLTE (second syllable rhymes with BOLT)

The family of German origin came to Charleston in the 1790s. As a fourteen-year-old Christopher Happoldt (1823–1878) served as secretary to John Bachman, John James Audubon's collaborator, during his 1838 trip to visit the Audubons in England and to attend an international science gathering in Germany. *The Christopher Happoldt Journal* (1960) is a record of this trip, with biographies of Bachman and Happoldt. A first-honor graduate of the Medical College of South Carolina, Happoldt studied further in Paris and Berlin and was editor of the internationally acclaimed *Charleston Medical Journal.* After serving as surgeon in the Confederate Army, he volunteered to combat yellow fever epidemics in Memphis and then in Vicksburg, where he died of the disease. Christopher's cousin, Dr. John Michael Happoldt, was such an ardent Southerner that, having no sons, he named his daughter Mary John C. Calhoun Happoldt.

Harllee
HAH-LEE

The forebear of this Peedee area family was Colonel Thomas H. Harllee, who came from Virginia in 1790 and established a store in what is now Dillon County. The town that grew up there was originally called Harlleeville; now it is Little Rock (SC 9 and SC

57), just west of the Little Peedee River. William Wallace Harllee (1812–1897), attorney, served as a major in the Seminole War (1837) and as a senator from Marion. He declined to run for governor in order to organize the Peedee Legion, Confederate States of America, which he commanded as brigadier general. In 1889 he named the town of Florence (US 52 and US 76) for his daughter. The general's brother Robert Harllee (1807–1872) served in the state House and Senate and was a physician and planter at Melrose Plantation near Mars Bluff (US 76, seven miles east of Florence). John Harllee, CPA and University of South Carolina graduate, has written articles and notes on place names in the Florence area for *Names in South Carolina* since his undergraduate days in Professor Neuffer's writing class.

Hartzog
HAHRT-zug

Hartzog Lane in Clemson is named for Henry S. Hartzog, president of Clemson College, 1897–1902. Benjamin Gerard Hartzog, Columbia attorney, was born in 1904 on his family's plantation— a land grant in the old Barnwell District to the German family in 1736. Isaac Hartzog remembers the naming of his native town of Hilda, for which his father gave the land for the railroad depot. The construction engineer of the Atlantic Coastline Railroad requested that the town be named for his sweetheart, and it was. When the railroad was finished he and Hilda, then his wife, rode through on one of the first passenger trains that connected Augusta, Barnwell, and Florence.

Hasell
HAZE-ul (like hazel)

The Rev. Thomas Hasell came from England in 1709 as the first rector of the Parish of St. Thomas in what is now lowcountry Berkeley County. His home was Pompion Hill Plantation near Pompion Hill Chapel—pronounced PUNGK-in locally by the learned and unlearned alike. Hasell Street in Sumter was named in 1905 by the mayor, Dr. George W. Dick, for his son Hasell Dick. There is also a Hasell Street in Charleston. The family is presently well-known in Columbia. Dr. Hasell Ross, Columbia physician, though not related to the family, was named for Hasell Thomas, whom Dr. Ross's father much revered. The name is often mispronounced HAS-ul and misspelled Hazel or even Hassel.

Haughabook
HAWK-uh-BOOK (OO as in foot)

Haughabook Swamp is crossed by Congaree, Thom's, and Dry creeks. Congaree Creek drains into the Congaree River about seven miles south of Columbia. Variously spelled Haughabook, Haughaboch, Haugaboo, Hogiboo, Huckabuck, and Hoggibou, the name also has various reputed origins from Norse legends or Indian tribes. Most often it is reported as deriving from Hagenbuch, the German family which settled nearby. Miss Webert Haughabook, the last of the line, was lost on a trip through the swamp that now bears her family's name, however misspelled.

Havilah
HAV-i-lah, huh-VIE-luh

South Carolinians called him HAV-i-lah (as down here did he himself); his wife Alice and folks in his native Appomatox, Virginia, called him huh-VIE-luh. Havilah Babcock (1898–1964) was a nationally acclaimed writer of hunting and fishing tales, head of University of South Carolina Department of English, and teacher of English for 38 years. His course, English 129, "I Want a Word" (vocabulary and semantics), was the most popular course on the Columbia campus. Students would sign up as much as a year in advance to be assured of places. But his love of hunting was such that, according to campus legend, when hunting season opened in November a sign was posted on his classroom door, "Doctor Babcock will be sick all next week." The excellence of his writing is evident in the first of his four books of collected short stories, *My Health Is Better in November*. The Havilah Babcock

Memorial Scholarship was established in 1969 by his students and friends to recognize student excellence in creative writing each year.

Heineman
HIE-nuh-mun

The little town of Heineman is no more. In Williamsburg County four miles west of Lane (SC 377, south of US 521), it was formerly a post office and flag stop for the Seaboard Coastline Railroad from Lane to Sumter. John Heineman, German musician, came to the area in the late 1800s, bought land, and built his home there. His grandson John Heineman served in the state House of Representatives in the 1970s from Georgetown.

Heise
HISE-si (rhymes with icy)

Heise's Pond, a popular swimming area in the 1930s for Columbia folk, is now part of Fort Jackson. Its generous owner was Richland County Sheriff Alex Heise. John H. Heise came from Germany to Georgetown about 1800. His son John H. Heise, Jr., born in Georgetown, came to Columbia in 1832 and established Heise's Retail and Wholesale Candy Manufacture. Also a caterer, he was known as "an Artist in Sugar." The name survives. Dr. Edward Alex Heise lives in Sumter. Philip Heise lives in Cayce (across the Congaree River from Columbia).

Heisman
HISE-mun (first syllable rhymes with ICE)

Heisman Street in Clemson is named for the Clemson College football coach (1900–1903) and Shakespearean actor John Heisman (1869–1936), whose Tigers trounced Georgia Tech 75–0. He is more nationally known for his innovations in the sport and for the prestigious Heisman Trophy awarded annually by the Downtown Athletic Club of New York (it was awarded to the University of South Carolina's George Rogers in 1980).

Helena
HEL-e-nuh

St. Helena's Island in the Beaufort Archipelago was named by the Spanish who reputedly landed there on August 13, 1520—St. Elena's Day on the Roman Catholic Church calendar. St. Helena's Sound is fed by the Ashepoo, Combahee, and Edisto rivers. In nearby St. Helena's Parish the Chapel of Ease was often called the White Church: it was made of oyster shells and lime (called tabby), built before the Revolution, and destroyed by fire some years after the Confederate War. The suburban town of Helena in the Dutch Fork area of Newberry County was originally the area for the railroad maintenance shops. It was named for Mrs. Helena O'Neall by her husband, John Belton O'Neall, who was attorney for the Columbia and Greenville Railroad, and author of *Biographical Sketches of the Bench and Bar of South Carolina* (1859) and co-author with John Chapman of *The Annals of Newberry* (1892).

Herendine
HEHR-en-din

Herendine Prong is a branch of Naked Creek in east Bennettsville (US 401 and SC 9) in the northeastern county of Marlboro. Recent maps incorrectly record it as Herndon Branch. The name originally was for a settler named Harrington (1793). The present spelling in Bennettsville is Herendine.

Hoefer
HAE-fuh

The Hoefer family, of German origin, are longtime residents of the Midlands. Frederick Augustus Hoefer came to South Carolina in 1840 and served in the Confederate army. Mrs. Jean Hoefer Toal, Columbia attorney, is one of the most active state legislators and has represented Richland County in the House since 1975. Herbert W. Hoefer is a member of the Columbia Landmark Commission.

Hofwyl
HAWF-wile

Hofwyl was an outstanding academy of learning (1853–1871), located a mile northwest of what is now the town of Latta (US 301 and SC 917) in the northeastern county of Dillon.

Honea
HUN-neh-uh

Honea Path (US 76 and 178) is a little town in upcountry Anderson County between Anderson and Laurens. Honea has been variously recorded as a family name (some say the postmaster's), as an Indian word meaning path (therefore redundant?), or as a distortion of Honey, referring to the many honeybees along the path. It is a fact that the town was chartered in 1855 as Honey Path, and then registered in 1877 with the present name Honea Path.

Horger

HUHR-guh

The Horgers, of German origin, were early settlers in the Orangeburg District. Several have been prominent physicians in the Midlands. Dr. Richard Culler Horger, born in 1917 in Eutawville, is a physician in Orangeburg.

Horlbeck

HAWL-BAK

Peter and John Horlbeck were architects of the Exchange Building, scene of Charleston's belligerent tea party, held in the broad daylight of high noon in October 1775—two months before Boston's much more history-book publicized, Indian-disguised sneak attack at night. Horlbeck Alley in Charleston leads from Meeting Street to Archdale. It was at a tavern at Horlbeck Alley and King Street that Ohio-born folklorist and writer John Bennett of the Charleston Poetry Society used to meet with Francis Nipson, who told him Gullah tales and legends over a few glasses of beer. Major John S. Horlbeck owned a large plantation in Christ Church Parish which had formerly been the residence of the Rutledge family. The family cemetery in the corner of a field caused the major to warn his plowman, "Now don't plow too close over to that section. High-class people are buried there."

Horrell

HAH-rul

Horrell Hill is a rural community some ten miles east of Columbia on US 76 (Garner's Ferry Road or Sumter Highway). Myers Hill was the original name, for William and Frederick Myers who owned land there. The first Richland County courthouse is reputed to have been built at Myers Hill in 1794. By mid-nineteenth century Thomas Horrell and his son lived at the foot of the hill—hence the present name Horrell Hill.

Horry
OH-REE

The northern coastal county of Horry is named for Revolutionary Colonel Peter Horry. Settled by small farmers, the county
is still referred to as "The Independent Republic of Horry." The
colonel and five others of the Horry family have represented the
lowcountry in the state Senate. The colonel moved to Columbia,
where he and his wife Margaret Guignard lived in what is now
called the Horry-Guignard House (northwest corner of Senate
and Pickens streets). Two stories evidence the too-often incorrect
pronunciation of Horry. Novelist Drayton Mayrant's mother, as a
schoolgirl, was laughed at by her classmates and kept in after
school because she refused to pronounce Colonel Peter Horry's
name to rhyme with *sorry*. She knew better; Pete was a forebear
of hers. And the other story is of Northern visitors. With their
guidebook for a walking tour of Charleston, they were looking in
vain for Colonel Horry's house. Seeing an old nurse walking her
little aristocratic charges along the Battery, the lead visitor sought
assistance: "Pardon, could you tell us where the HOH-ri House
is?" Quick was the old nurse's indignant reply: "Don't you dare
talk dat way in front of dese chillun. Dis is a 'spectable neighborhood. What you looking fah is over on Beresford Street." The Big
Brick for years was the notorious house of prostitution on Beresford Street. When it was torn down some years ago, city council
changed the name of the street because of past association. After
much discussion, Beresford became Fulton Street—the only reason
being that a bust of Robert Fulton happened to be on a shelf in
the room where council was meeting. (Sam Stoney, the Mr.
Charleston of South Carolina historians, is our source for this
Horry story.)

Howie
HOW-i

Thomas D. Howie, Abbeville born and reared, is beloved by the
liberated French of World War II as "The Major of St. Lo." His
statue and a Howie Boulevard in the little town of St. Lo attest

to the citizens' appreciation. Howie's battalion led the assault that drove the Germans from the long-occupied town. In the forefront of the attack, the Major gave his life for the victory. The family name still survives in the upcountry.

Howle

OWL

It's a family name in the Peedee section (Darlington County). The area is called Birdland because of the family names of several residents—Byrd, Hawkins, Howle, and Sparrow.

Huger

YOO-JEE (OO as in booze)

The town, ferry, and street names over the state, but concentrated in the lowcountry, are often incorrectly pronounced HUE-juhr, HUE-JEE, or HUG-guhr. It's a French Huguenot family name, which two hundred years ago might have been pronounced something like YOO-ZHAE. But in South Carolina it has long been YOO-JEE, as a descendant recently wrote us: "I well remember our linens being carefully marked in a red thread *U.G.*" Major Benjamin Huger of North Island (off Georgetown) entertained Lafayette there when he first landed in America in 1775. There is a Huger Drive in Georgetown. Isaac Huger was a Revolutionary general. In 1786 he had a ferry at his plantation on the Congaree River below Columbia in what is now the Beidler Tract of the Great Congaree Swamp. There is a Huger Street named for him in the commercial area of Columbia which provides continual argument over the pronunciation by tradesmen, customers, and media broadcasters. Even in Charleston, to the request for the number of D. Huger Bacot, a telephone operator searched in vain and responded, "I'm sorry, sir; we don't have a listing for Dug Bacot." (After the name was spelled, she found it.)

Huggins
HUG-inz, HUE-ginz

Mrs. Katie Huggins Hennecy, originally from Mullins (US 76 and SC 57) in the Peedee section, pronounces her maiden name HUG-inz. Mrs. Cornelia Huggins Hensley of Columbia pronounces her maiden name HUE-ginz. The family name is found throughout the state, pronounced either way, according to the person's preference.

Huguenin
HUE-guh-nin

Some Huguenins say they are French Huguenots; others, German-speaking Swiss. Early families settled on the coast in old Beaufort; later ones settled in lower Richland. Edward P. Huguenin, Jr., of Ridgeland (I 95 and US 17) is a farmer and former superintendent of education.

Inabinet
in-NAB-in-net

The Inabinet family (also spelled Inabinett and Inabinette) were German Swiss who came to the Orangeburg District around 1740. The name is now found throughout the state. E. L. (Les) Inabinet is director of the University of South Carolina's Caroliniana Library (on the Columbia Campus) and secretary of its supporting society.

iodine
IE-deen, IE-DINE

In the 1930s South Carolina was widely publicized as the Iodine State. Dr. William Weston, director of the state's Natural Resources Commission, promoted our fruits and vegetables for their richness in natural iodine, essential for the prevention of goiter. Columbia's WIS radio station, founded at that time, selected its call letters to represent Wonderful Iodine State, beating out a Wisconsin radio station that also wanted those letters.

'Ion

IE-un

'Ion Avenue on Sullivan's Island is a residential street named for Colonel Jacob Bond 'Ion, veteran of the Mexican War. A jolly dispenser of hospitality (he was affectionately called "Fat Uncle"), his home was a favorite gathering place for officers from nearby Fort Moultrie. One of his most frequent visitors was a red-haired lieutenant named William T. Sherman. The colonel's name is frequently written I'on, but in his will and in family papers it is 'Ion. Irons Cross Roads in Colleton County is about six miles southwest of Cottageville at roads 40 and 45; the place name is a corruption of the family name 'Ion to I'ons and then to Irons. The Colonel (1782–1859), and his father, Jacob Bond 'Ion (1746–1796), both served their country in war and their state in the Senate. Both are buried at Hobcaw on the Wando River.

Ioor

YOHR (as in days of yore)

The name is of Dutch origin, sometimes spelled Joor, and may mean earth. Ioor family members were among the Dorchester, Massachusetts, puritans who came to the Charleston vicinity in 1695. Some of the puritans and this unusual name were left behind when the Dorchester group moved on to middle Georgia. Dr. William Ioor was the first native South Carolinian to compose a professionally produced play: *Independence* was first performed March 30, 1805, in Charleston. Two others of his plays, *The Battle of Eutaw Springs* and *The Evacuation of Charleston*, were produced in 1807. After practicing medicine in his native St. George's Parish near Old Dorchester and in Savannah, Georgia, Dr. Ioor moved to lower Greenville District around 1820. As a descendant has reported, "he had become impoverished by trying to maintain Low Country traditions of hospitality and sought refuge in the less luxurious Up Country." His wife was one of the founders of Christ Episcopal Church in Greenville. Raven Ioor McDavid, Greenville descendant of the doctor-playwright, has been a prominent scholar, writer, and director of the Linguistic Atlas at the University of Chicago. Mrs. Clint T. (Raven Simkins) Graydon of Columbia was also a Ioor descendant. Another prominent physician, teacher, and historian, Dr. Joseph Ioor Waring of Charleston's Old Town, also bore the interesting name.

Irmo

UHR-MOE

The Lexington County town of Irmo is west of Columbia on SC 60 off I 26 near Lake Murray. It is not Indian; and it has nothing to do with the "ancient Irmese," as in the fun-poking allegations by WSCQ's morning showman Gene McKay. The name Irmo was derived by combining the first two letters of the surnames of C. J. Iredell of Columbia and H. C. Moseley of Prosperity. They were founding officials of the Columbia, Newberry and Laurens Railroad. Recent industrialization in the area has fostered mammoth residential development in and around Irmo.

Isaqueena

IS-uh-KWEE-nuh

Isaqueena Falls and Creek are in Oconee, the northwestern most county of the state, a few miles northwest of the town of Walhalla (SC 28 and SC 107). Isaqueena was the fictional Choctaw name for the fictional Cherokee Indian maiden Cateechee. The lengthy poem *Cateechee of Keowee* (1898) by Dr. James Walter Daniel, is documented "proof" of her existence still accepted by many. (See Cateechee.) It was at Isaqueena Falls, according to the legend, that the Indian maiden and her white lover, clasped in each other's arms, leapt to their deaths to escape the wrath of the Cherokees she had betrayed.

Jalapa
juh-LAP-puh

The pronunciation is obviously Carolinized. The little town of
Jalapa (off I 26, on US 76) seven miles northwest of Newberry
has a Spanish language origin from the Mexican War (1848). Re-
turning from battle, members of the Palmetto Regiment stopped
off in Newberry County, where the pleasant area reminded them
of the Mexican city of Jalapa (hu-LAH-puh to Mexican speakers),
whose residents had been so hospitable. It was these soldiers—
called "The Tigers" by General Winfield Scott, because they were
such fierce fighters—who gave the name Jalapa to the town.

jasmine, jessamine
JAS-min, JES-uh-min

Yellow Jessamine (a native wild and often domesticated vine with
inverted bell-shaped blooms) is the state flower (*Gelsemium
sempervirens*). Officially spelled jessamine, sometimes it is also
given the phonetic spelling, jasmine. Cape jasmine is the local
name for our most popular gardenia (*Gardenia jasminoides*),
named in honor of South Carolina naturalist Dr. Alexander Garden (1731–1790). Born in Scotland, Doctor Garden came to
Georgetown in 1750, practiced medicine in Charleston, and was
internationally recognized for his work in botany. The popular
name cape jasmine was derived from the misimpression that the
plant was native to the Cape of Good Hope, South Africa; actually
it was native to China.

Jeremy
JEH-ri-mi

Jeremy Island in Charleston County is bordered by the Inland
Waterway and the marshes of DuPre and Clubhouse creeks. It
was plantation land belonging to the Seewee Indian Chief Jeremy,
from whom it took its name. Natives of McClellanville (off US 17

on SC 45) often refer to their town as "The Village"—short for its older name, the Village of Jeremy Creek.

Jervey
JUHR-vi

David Jervey, founder of the family in South Carolina, came from Scotland to Charleston prior to 1738. His son, Thomas, a broker and merchant, was a Captain in the Continental Army during the Revolution. The name is sometimes pronounced juhr-VAE and confused with Gervais by newcomers to the state. Dr. J. P. Jervey was among the prominent members (including also Dr. F. Y. Porcher, James Louis Petigru, and Henry Grimké) of the Clay Political Club, which promoted the Whig candidate Henry Clay for President against the Nullifier and native son John C. Calhoun. William R. Jervey of Summerville, and later Columbia minister of the African Methodist Episcopal Church, served in the South Carolina House and Senate (1868–1872) during Reconstruction. Thomas Dehon Jervey (born 1877) wrote a biography of Robert Y. Hayne (1909), a history, *The Slave Trade* (1925), and a novel on South Carolina Reconstruction, *The Elder Brother* (1905). W. Thomas Jervey, native Columbian of David Jervey descent, was recently trust officer of the University of South Carolina's Educational Foundation. Mr. and Mrs. Jervey D. Royal are active in the Poetry Society of South Carolina.

Jeter
JEET-uh

The Jeter House in Union (US 176 and SC 49) in the northwestern part of the state was the home of Thomas Bothwell Jeter (1827–1883). A lawyer, he served in the state House and Senate and as governor. Other Jeter men who served in both the House and Senate were John Speed Jeter (1779–1847), lawyer and solicitor from Edgefield (US 25 and SC 23); and James Thomas Jeter (1867–1940), physician and planter from Santuck (SC 215, southeast of Union), who was also a captain in the medical corps in World War I. Pat Jeter, University of South Carolina campus beauty of the early 1940s, pronounced her name JET-uh; her sister Lois, at Columbia College, gave in to the local pronunciation and answered to JEET-uh. Their Jeter family was from Indiana, where their name was pronounced JET-uhr. The Jeter name and JEET-uh pronunciation still survive in the state.

Joanna
JOE-AN-nuh

The little mill town in Laurens County at US 76 and SC 66 has had varied names during the past 150 years: Milton, a stagecoach stop; Martin's Depot, changed to avoid confusion with another Martin's; Goldville, because a farmer there just before the Civil War sold so much cotton at a high price that he seemed to be growing gold; and the present name, since about 1950, for the Joanna Western Company, which owns and operates the textile mill there.

Jocassee
JOE-KAS-si

Jocassee lake, valley, and town are located in the northwestern corner of the state in Oconee County near the Whitewater River close by the Pickens County line. For 37 years Camp Jocassee was operated as a vacation area for girls by Sarah Ellerbe Godbold (1898–1979), feared and beloved physical education teacher in Columbia area colleges and the old Columbia High School at the corner of Washington and Marion streets. Jocassee is an Indian word maybe meaning an impish sprite, helpful to hunters but often tricking them into falling. Novelist William Gilmore Simms interpreted the name of the Cherokee princess to mean "full-bosom or fertile field." When she saw the scalp of her white lover dangling from the neck of his Indian conqueror, Princess Jocassee threw herself into the river (now a lake) that bears her name.

Jordan
JAWD-un, JUHRD-un

Thomas Jordan, from Ireland, was a resident of the northwest county of Abbeville according to the 1790 census. The community of Jordan, named for a resident family in lowcountry Clarendon County, is a few miles south of the county seat of Manning on the road to Lake Marion. James Jordan from Spartanburg and Oliver Cromwell Jordan from Aiken served in the state House and Senate in the 1890s. The pronunciation is left to family preference, though in South Carolina it is more often JAWD-un. Hamilton, the Georgia aide to ex-President Carter, answers to JUHRD-un; Columbia pharmacist Leonard prefers JAWD-un; and Abbeville's Jordan Ramey was called both.

Jumelle
juh-MEL

Jumelle Hill is a suburb of beautiful homes in the Midlands town of Camden (US 1, northeast of Columbia). Pierre Laurent Jumelle came to Camden from Santo Domingo following the black rebellion on that island in 1793. In the Kershaw County town he operated a dancing school, where he taught dancing, social graces, and refined manners characteristic of the French. He built his home on the hill that now bears his name.

Keitt
KIT

Some Keitt families pronounce the name KEET, but most prefer KIT. Keitt's Crossroads was the old name for the intersection of US 176 and SC 34 in Newberry County. Local folks explain, "That's near the old Joe Keitt house," though descendants of earliest settlers resent the use of *old* for the Keitt folks, who came a bit later. The Keitts have long been a prominent family in Amelia Township, later called Calhoun County, southeast of Columbia.

Congressman Lawrence M. Keitt accompanied Congressman Preston S. Brooks in 1856 when he caned Senator Charles Sumner for ridiculing Brooks's cousin, Senator Andrew Pickens Butler, on the floor of the U.S. Senate. The same Lawrence M. Keitt was the commanding colonel of the Twentieth South Carolina Infantry in the Confederate War. Eartha Keitt, black singer of national renown, was born in the Orangeburg County town of North (US 321 and US 178), later moved to Harlem, and changed the spelling of her name to Kitt.

Keowee
KEE-uh-WEE

The chief village of the Cherokee Indians was at the northwest head of the Cherokee Path in Oconee County. The old town is now under the waters of Lake Keowee belonging to the Duke Power Company. The present nearby town of Keowee is on US 123, two miles west of Clemson. The Indian name, possibly meaning "mulberry-grove place," is also used locally for the weekly newspaper the *Keowee Courier*, published by Jack L. Hunt at Walhalla, county seat of Oconee, and for the Keowee River. The covered bridge built in 1916 across the river used 5,000 feet of heart pine from the area and is named Chapman's Bridge for earlier settlers, descendants of whom helped to build it. Other Chapmans still live there. It is also called Craig's Bridge, for James B. Craig, Pickens County road supervisor at the time of its construction.

Kerr
KAHR, KUHR (like a car or curr)

The family name Kerr dates back at least to Robert Kerr of Scotland in 1340. Davis Kerr came from Virginia to the Abbeville District (northwestern part of the state) in 1762. In the Revolution he fought at King's Mountain and in the siege of Ninety Six, and he helped to capture an Indian town and a Tory fort. Kerr's Wharf in Charleston, from East Bay to the Cooper River at the foot of

Queen Street, was purchased by Thomas J. Kerr in 1854 from William Patton. The late Davis ("Son") Kerr, prominent Spartanburg attorney, pronounced his name KAHR. Some families have accepted the phonetic KUHR.

Kershaw
KUHR-SHAW

Joseph Kershaw and William Ancrum were the founders of Camden (1733), northeast of Columbia on US 1. Kershaw was one of the most prominent men of his day in Camden District—a legislator, administrator of public affairs, and colonel in the Revolution —and the district was given his name when it became a county. Three different Kershaws have served as mayor of Camden. The town of Kershaw (US 521 and US 601), north of Camden, is named for another family member, Joseph Brevard Kershaw, who was a major general in the Confederate Army.

Keyserling
KIE-zuhr-ling

Mrs. B. Herbert (Harriet H.) Keyserling is a member of the state House of Representatives from Beaufort.

Kiawah
KEE-ah-WAH

This Sea Island south of Charleston is one of the few which have retained their Indian names. The friendly Kiawahs were the tribe which encouraged the first English colonists to settle in Charleston (1670) rather than in Beaufort. Kiawah Island was granted in 1699 to George Raynor, who may have been a pirate. In 1719 it was purchased from Raynor's grandson by John Stanyarne, who built the Vanderhorst House, the mansion that still stands there, and successfully planted indigo on the island. The house is named for the Vanderhorsts, the descendants of one of Stanyarne's granddaughters, Elizabeth Raven, and Adolphus Vanderhorst II. The family was known as the "kings of Kiawah." In 1974 the island was bought by the Kuwait Investment Corporation; it has been developed into a resort.

Kibler
KIB-luh

Kibler's Bridge in central Newberry County is the Southern Railway span across the deep valley south of SC 773 and west of I 26. The area was earlier called Kibler's, then Kibler's Station, named for the German Kübler family that had settled in the area by 1766. Before 1836 David Kibler (1802–1882) moved from Kibler's to Frog Level (since 1873 called Prosperity; US 76 and SC 391), where he was a farmer, merchant, and the first postmaster. Among the many undocumented explanations of the origin of the name Frog Level this is the best story: A man with a jug reeled through the area on a mule. When he had drunk all the spirits, he and the jug fell off the mule and rolled into a ditch. When a gulley-washing rain brought him to, he saw a frog croaking on the edge of the ditch above him, and he was very ashamed. "I've been low in my time, but this is the first time I've been below frog level." He straightened up, became a proper citizen, and henceforth the town nearby was called Frog Level. The town celebrated its centennial as Prosperity in 1973; J. Walter Hamm is the mayor. Professor James Kibler, of the University of Georgia English Department and descendant of David, the first postmaster of Frog Level, summons up remembrance of things past and says maybe he'll retire early from teaching, go back to Prosperity, get the name changed back to Frog Level, and become another Kibler postmaster.

Killian
KIL-yun

The town of Killian is in northeast Richland County on SC 555. The town is named for the Killian family, and it is misspelled KILLAN on the official election map.

Kinard
KINE-ud

The Newberry County town of Kinards (US 76, west of Chapin) in the Dutch Fork section is named for the Kinard family among the early German settlers. It was first called Kinard Hill. John Kinard, who lived there, gave each of his sons land on which to build his home. By 1860 Martin Kinard was one of the area's most prosperous planters and largest slave owners (he had 106). Huggins Ferry in nearby Saluda in the 1930s was sometimes called Kinards Ferry. The Kinard name is still prominent in the Midlands: Lutheran minister James C. Kinard was president of Newberry College. John P. Kinard was a state senator. Dr. Frederick William Kinard was a faculty member of the state medical college. Minister Karl William Kinard was president of the Lutheran Synod. Thomas Burney Kinard, Jr., is a Columbia attorney. The outstanding black Clemson football player Terry Kinard pronounces his name kuh-NAHRD.

Kinloch
KIN-law

The Kinloch family came from Scotland to the Colonial lowcountry. The black family of similar name in the state today spells and pronounces the name Kinlock (KIN-lok). Kinloch Creek, flowing into the North Santee River southwest of Georgetown, was named for Francis Kinloch, who owned nearby Rice Hope Plantation. Belvidere Plantation, now at the bottom of Lake Marion, was the home of his father, James Kinloch, as early as 1725. Acton Plantation in Stateburg (off US 378 on SC 261) in Sumter County was owned and named by Cleland Kinloch. It was purchased in 1906 by Colonel John J. Dargan, who operated General Sumter Memorial Academy there. Kinloch Court (now Philadelphia Street or Cow Alley) in Charleston, according to a *News and Courier* account, "was the scene of a duel one bright Sunday morning when General William Moultrie pinked his man in beauty's quarrel. When the General had run his sword through his opponent's arm, he immediately withdrew it, wiped the blade, and after courteously saluting his antagonist, turned the corner and attended divine services at St. Philip's Church." John Kinloch Rivers is a poet and counselor in the Charleston city schools.

Kinsler
KIN-sluh

As early as 1731 Conrad Kinsler (German Künsler) had land grants on the Broad River and upper Cedar Creek in upper Richland County north of Columbia. The land is still owned by his descendants. Captain John Kinsler served in the Revolution under Colonel William Thomson and was killed by a Tory while recovering from a wound received at the Battle of Fish Dam Ferry. The Mills Atlas of 1820 shows the Kinsler home on high ground between Burgess Creek and Kinsler Branch (now Slate Stone Branch), which crosses Monticello Road (SC 215) about one mile below Burgess Creek. The many Kinsler descendants in the Midlands include Beckham, Bookman, Davis, LaBorde, Marshall, Nelson, and Sligh families, according to *The Kinslers of South Carolina* (1964) by W. Kinsler Beckham.

Klugh
KLOO (OO as in booze)

Humphrey Klugh (1760–1837) came from Virginia to old Ninety Six District (northeast of Greenwood) in 1792. James Coke Klugh (1857–1911) was a Greenwood teacher, Abbeville lawyer, and circuit judge. His home on Wardlaw Street is on the annual Abbeville Historical Tour begun in 1978. Klugh Avenue in upstate Clemson (US 123 and US 76) is named for William Wightman Klugh, a member of Clemson College's first graduating class and later a professor of drawing at the college.

Kohn
KONE, KAHN

Usually the Protestant Kohn is pronounced KAHN, and the Jewish KONE. For many years in mid-twentieth-century Columbia, Kohn's (pronounced KONEZ) was a fashionable women's clothing store on Main Street. At the same time there were also August Kohn (KONE), financier, and Miss Erin Kohn (KAHN), writer and doll collector. David Kohn was author of the history, *Internal Improvements in South Carolina* (1938). The similar German name Kuhn has also been spelled Kahun, Coon, and Koon and is pronounced KOON, as in raccoon. Caspar Kuhn was a Swiss German immigrant of 1739, first to Orangeburg, then to upper Richland County's Crane Creek section. He had three sons—Adam, Conrad, and Lewis. In the area there was a Koon Town and a Koon Road (now US 21).

Kolb
KULP

Kolb was a prominent family name in the Welsh Neck section of the Peedee area's present Marlboro County before the Revolution. Abel Kolb married Sarah James, who owned a plantation on the Peedee River. He ran Kolb Ferry, crossing the Peedee north of the present bridge to Society Hill (US 401 and US 52, south of Cheraw). A colonel in the Revolution, Abel Kolb was killed by tories on April 28, 1781.

Kuykendall
KUHRK-en-DAWL

It's a York County family name. Dr. William Kuykendall, professor of archeology at Erskine College, always instructed his students at the first class meeting to pronounce his name with the first syllable as in the family name of Francis Marion Kirk, rhyming with *jerk*.

LaBorde
luh-BOHRD

This one was included when we heard a radio newscaster say "luh-BODE dormitory." Not all Southerners leave out all r sounds. The first Pierre LaBorde, from Bordeaux, France, came to Charleston from Santo Domingo in 1793, following the insurrection there, and then moved to Edgefield. His son, Maximilian LaBorde, M.D., was honor graduate, trustee, professor, and president of South Carolina College. One of the high-rise dormitories whose exterior resembles a honeycomb on the Columbia campus is named for this "professor who saved Carolina from Sherman's torch." Dr. Jean B. LaBorde owns his great-grandfather's dueling pistols with which the professor supposedly held off "the whole Yankee army"; the more conservative say he did it with effective rhetoric; others say "with his squirrel rifle." Maximilian LaBorde also served in the legislature, was South Carolina's secretary of state, and is the only layman to be honored with a memorial plaque in Trinity Episcopal Cathedral, of which he was for forty years senior warden. He wrote the first history of South Carolina College, a medical textbook, and two novelettes. He was one of the first doctors to promote occupational therapy for the mentally ill, and LaBorde Building at the state mental hospital is named for him. Maximilian's descendants are four generations of medical doctors, four University of South Carolina professors, and other teachers, lawyers, engineers, and executives.

Lachicotte
LASH-uh-KOT

The French family fled Santo Domingo in 1792 during the slave rebellion there, and sailed for Philadelphia. In 1805 they moved to Charleston. Their name has undergone an interesting evolution. Originally it was Rossignol, but on Santo Domingo this branch of the family added the name of their plantation: Rossignol–La Chicotte. In America it was abbreviated to LaChicotte or Lachicotte. The present family in coastal Georgetown County almost swallows (elides) the middle syllable so that the casual listener might hear only LASH-KOT. Waverly, the Allston family plantation, became the property of Philip R. Lachicotte in 1871. About the same time Lachicotte families owned three of the twelve oldest houses on Pawley's Island. In 1938 Arthur Herbert Lachicotte founded the famous Pawley's Island Hammock Shop, specializing in handmade rope hammocks, originated by his brother-in-law, Joshua John Ward. It is now a veritable shopping center on US 17 (the King's Highway, from Charleston through the Grand Strand). Alberta Morel Lachicotte wrote the history, *Georgetown Rice Plantations* (1955). Waverly Rice Mills, founded by her great-grandfather, was operated by the Lachicotte family until 1911. Lewis Lachicotte, longtime twentieth-century Columbia jeweler, had a store on Main Street. The Lachicotte Medal in Music Excellence is awarded annually at Converse College in Spartanburg.

Lady's
LADE-iz

Lady's Island, the northwest section of St. Helena's Island in the Beaufort Archipelago, is included not to correct its pronunciation so much as its too frequent misspelling, Ladies. One story reports its being named by the Spanish for Our Lady, Mother of Christ, when they claimed the land for Spain in 1525 on Our Lady's day of the Roman Catholic Church calendar. But over two hundred years later some 3,000 acres on the island came into the possession of Lady Elizabeth Blake. By act of the British

House of Commons in 1740 the island was named for Lady Elizabeth. Whether the origin of the name is religious or aristocratic, it's single and possessive, not plural.

LaFaye
luh-FIE

From Bordeaux, France, the family migrated to Louisiana and came to Columbia in the early twentieth century. The brothers, George and Robert, established the architectural firm of LaFaye and LaFaye, prominent in the development of Wales Gardens homes in Columbia and other residences and commercial buildings in the Midlands. Nell LaFaye, an artist on the University of South Carolina faculty, wonders if the family name might originally have been LaFayette.

LaFitte
luh-FEET

The Santo Domingan French name, spelled LaFitte, Laffitte, and Lafite, is still present, especially in Columbia, Saluda, Estill, and Allendale. In 1866 Lafitte brothers owned the old Patton Wharf at the foot of Hasell Street in Charleston. John LaFitte of Columbia served in the legislature and on Governor James B. Edwards' staff, 1974–1978 (Edwards was the first Republican governor in the state since Reconstruction). Henry Lucius Laffitte is a physician in Estill. But the most notorious bearer of the name was not a South Carolinian. Jean Laffitte (or Lafitte), who lived from about 1780 to about 1825, was a smuggler and pirate, operating off the coast of Louisiana and Texas.

Lamar
luh-MAH

This Peedee town is on US 401, south of I 20 in Darlington County. Lamar has been named Devil's Woodyard, Mims Crossroads for a merchant there, Lisbon in 1872, and its present name, in 1886, for Mississippian Lucius Quintus Cincinnatus Lamar (1825–1893), member of President Grover Cleveland's Cabinet and Supreme Court Justice. The Lamar Riots of the 1970s involved opposition to court-ordered integration of public schools by busing. Thomas Lamar, forebear of Mrs. A. S. Salley, owned the plantation Airville Place in old Edgefield District (now Aiken County) on the Savannah River. Prominent Lamars today include Howard Henry Lamar, Jr., Greenville banker, and Elsie Nixon Lamar, former headmistress of Columbia's Heathwood Hall Episcopal School.

Lancaster

LANG-kus-tuh

Granted, Pennsylvania folk and the actor Burt Lancaster pronounce their name LAN-KAS-tuhr, but in South Carolina the town, county, and family name is LANG-kus-tuh. In 1785 the county along the North Carolina line was named by Scotch-Irish settlers from Lancaster, Pennsylvania. The town was originally called Barnettsville, but when chartered in 1802 the name was changed to Lancaster. James Boyd Lancaster of Pauline represented Union County in the state House and Senate, 1926–1938. And Harry Lancaster was a mighty sharp student at Satchel Ford School in Columbia in the 1960s before his family moved to Charlotte, North Carolina.

Landrum

LAN-drum

The town of Landrum is northeast of Greenville in Spartanburg County almost on the North Carolina line. It is named for John Gill Landrum. His father, Dr. J. B. O. Landrum, was a physician and writer of two upcountry histories. In the area of Greer (SC 14 off US 29) in Greenville County, Dr. Landrum's home, built in 1871, still stands. Landrum Road in Forest Acres (northeast of Columbia) is named for Dr. Abner Landrum, renowned maker

of whiteware and ornate pottery, who moved from Edgefield to
Columbia in 1830. His kiln on Bethel Church Road was closed
in 1965 by owner Raymond Stork, great-grandson of Doctor Landrum. The condominiums built on the surrounding land kept the
kiln chimney as a landmark, and the developers misnamed the
residences Brickyard Village—Doctor Landrum never made bricks.

Lanneau
luh-NOO (OO as in boot)

One of the most prominent of this French family was Basil Lanneau Gildersleeve (1831–1924), noted classical scholar and professor of Greek at the University of Virginia and Johns Hopkins
University. The late Dr. Chapman J. Milling, Darlington native
and long a resident of Columbia, was a descendant of Pierre
Lanneau, one of the founders of this distinguished family of
Charleston. Other notable Lanneaus were the Rev. John F. Lanneau and Basil Edward Lanneau, professor of Hebrew at the
Lutheran Theological Seminary in Columbia. Lanneau Foster
taught psychology at the University of South Carolina, operated
a widely known school of dance, and played championship chess.
How contrary to the proper French are our pronunciations of such
names as Lanneau and Lenud was delightfully limericked in a
letter to us back in the 1960s from novelist-poet Drayton Mayrant:

> I have heard of a strange interview
> Between Messrs le Nud and Lanneau.
>> Said the former "It's rude
>> To call me luh NUDE
> When I'm dressed. I pronounce it luh NOO."

> The latter agreed, "It is so.
> In la Belle France my name was luh NO.
>> So gladly to you
>> I will give the sound U
> If in turn you will rhyme me with beau."

Contrary to the original French, for the most part, the family and
the place names (as in Lanneau Drive in Greenville) have become
luh-NOO.

Laurens

LAH-renz

It takes a keen ear and careful tongue to distinguish between the pronunciations of Laurens (LAH-renz) and Lawrence (LAH-rins; also spelled Laurence). The upcountry town of Laurens (first called Laurensville) is south of US 276 on US 76 in Laurens County. One of South Carolina's most prominent national figures, Henry Laurens was president of the Continental Congress and one of the four Americans sent after the Revolution to draft and sign the Treaty of Paris, 1783. Mepkin Plantation on the Cooper River (near Moncks Corner and now the monastery of the Trappist Monks) was purchased by Henry Laurens in 1762 from John Colleton. Today the name Laurens is preserved as both a family name and a given name (male and female).

LeConte

luh-KONT

Some of our folks attempt to give the name an affected "French" pronunciation (loo-KONTE; oo as in foot), but the carriers of the name in these parts (*e.g.*, LeConte Gibbes and Louis Le-Conte of Columbia) answer to luh-KONT. Before the Civil War the LeConte brothers, John the physician and scientist and Joseph the physician and geologist, were professors at South Carolina College. They had previously taught at the University of Georgia and after the war went to the University of California. All three state universities have buildings named LeConte College for the renowned brothers. Joseph was also an expert mountain climber, and Mt. LeConte, the second highest mountain in the Great Smokies, and Mt. LeConte in Yosemite National Forest are named for him. The Brevard House, an 1800-acre plantation in the sandhills of lower Richland County, was owned in 1966 by Louis Le-Conte.

Legare
luh-GREE

The French pronunciation would be something like luh-gah-RAE. Although in no way related to Simon Legree, the cruel overseer of *Uncle Tom's Cabin*, the same un-French pronunciation is given to this Huguenot family name applied to a building, town, island, and streets over the state. Legare College, built in 1848 on the south side of the Horseshoe of Columbia's University of South Carolina campus, was named for Hugh Swinton Legare, attorney and Unionist who served as United States Secretary of State and Attorney General. Legareville, a village on the coastal Stono River, was burned by the Confederates in 1865 to prevent its being used by invading Union forces. Sol Legare Island is named for its former owner. The island, which once had a shipbuilding industry, is on the bend of the Stono River at the southwest tip of James Island. The Legare-Morgan House, on the National Register of Historic Places, is the second oldest house in Aiken (US 1, east of the Savannah River). It was built by James Mathewes Legare, poet, painter, and inventor, who died there in 1859. The residence was purchased in 1870 by Thomas Charles Morgan, a British naval officer, and is still owned by his descendants.

Leitner
LITE-nuh

The German family name, still present in the Midlands, is also spelled Leightner and Lightner. George and John Leitner settled in upper Richland County on Little River before the Revolution. The old family home was in a giant oak grove on a hill overlooking Shaver Creek. Leitner Branch (now Home Branch) crosses Monticello Road (SC 215) just before the road reaches Little River. Leitner Grove Church was on County Road 420 in the same area. Michal Leitner, born in 1734 probably in Pennsylvania, came to Newberry about 1752. He was a planter and a major in the Revolution. From Crims Creek in the Dutch Fork, he served in the state House and Senate. William Zachariah Leitner (1829–1888) represented Kershaw County in the state House and Senate. He was also a judge and South Carolina's secretary of state.

Lenud
luh-NOOD (OO as in boot)

The French pronunciation would be luh-NOO (see Lanneau).
This early Huguenot family settled in the lower Santee River area.
Lenud's Ferry, location of a Revolutionary battle, was in the low-
country where US 17A now crosses the Santee River.

Lesesne
luh-SANE

The Lesesne family was one of several French Huguenot groups
who moved from Charleston into the Williamsburg area. Three
Lesesne men have served in the state Senate: Peter Lesesne
(1772–1837) from St. Thomas and St. Dennis; Henry Deas Lesesne
(1811–1886) from Charleston; and James Henry Lesesne (1867–
1918) from Clarendon. Dr. Joab Mauldin Lesesne, born in Kingstree (US 52 and SC 527) of Williamsburg County, was a history
professor (1940–1954) and then president of Erskine College in
upcountry Due West, of which little town he also served as mayor.
Lesesne Creek (now called Seine Creek) begins at Murrell's Inlet
and runs to a point off Drunken Jack Island, where it forks into
Allston Creek north and Oak Channel south. Though *seine* is a
word associated with fishing and there is good fishing here, the
present name may result from the clipping off of the first syllable
of the former name, Lesesne Creek.

Leslie
LES-li

Some having Leslie as a first name prefer giving the z sound to
the s and pronounce their name LEZ-li, but the surname is generally pronounced LES-li. Leslie School in upcountry Greenwood
is named for James Leslie, one of the first and most prominent
male teachers in the area, according to Mrs. Martha McCabe, its
principal in 1973. The 1820 Mills Atlas shows William Leslie a

large landowner on Leslie Creek (now Calhoun Creek), three miles north of Abbeville Court House. His descendants (the James Leslie family) still live on this land. Obviously of another branch, the Barnwell resident Charles P. Leslie, came from New York as an employee of the Federal Revenue Department and served in the state House and Senate during Reconstruction (1868–1876), after which he left the state.

Lethe
LEE-th*i*

Lethe Plantation was across Little River from New Bordeaux in the upcountry's old Abbeville District. Established in 1785, Lethe is now the state-owned John De la Howe School. For the story of Lethe (meaning forgetfulness), its owner Dr. John De la Howe, and his housekeeper Rebecca Woodin, see "A Grave in the Wilderness," *State Magazine*, 24 January 1954; it would make a fascinating historical novel. Near Allendale on the Savannah River was another Lethe Plantation, owned by an intimate friend of Dr. De la Howe, Robert McIlwraith, chief armorer for South Carolina during the Revolution. Before 1820 the Allendale Lethe was owned by Isaac Bourdeaux, and part of it in 1972 was in the possession of the Wade B. Warren family.

Lever
LEE-vuh

For the family and the tool used with a fulcrum, most South Carolinians say LEE-vuh, not LE-vuhr. The Lever Community in upper Richland County off Monticello Road (SC 215) was named for the J. W. Lever family, which settled on a land grant there in 1747. Still in the Midlands, the Levers have long been politically prominent, serving in both state government and the U.S. Congress. For over half a century a stop at Lever's Barbecue has been a must for those who eat hearty of such on the Fourth of July, Labor Day, and at political stump meetings.

Levy, Levi, Leevi

LEE-VIE, LEE-vi

Although some pronounce the name LEE-vi, the Jewish family in Camden and Sumter answers to the equally accented LEE-VIE. Chapman Levy, attorney, served as a captain of a rifle company in the War of 1812. In 1833 a duel was fought in Camden between Captain Mordecai Levy and the Hon. John Hemphill of Camden and Chester. Hemphill was shot in the hand and unable to fire, so that the matter was deemed settled for all concerned. During World War I, Wendell M. Levi of Sumter was a first lieutenant in the Signal Corps. His training of carrier pigeons led to his writing *The Pigeon* (1941), an authoritative volume with 785 illustrations, which has been sold in 61 foreign countries. Isaac J. Levy (pronounced LEE-vi) is professor of Spanish at the Columbia campus of the University of South Carolina. Isaac Leevy (also pronounced LEE-vi), Columbia black, founded Leevy Funeral Home. His grandson, I. S. Leevy Johnson, Columbia attorney, served several terms in the state House of Representatives before retiring in 1980. Perhaps a variant spelling of the same name is the Leavy family of Blackville.

Lewie

LOO-i (OO as in booze)

When used as a given name the family name is often misinterpreted as a nickname for Lewis. General Lewie G. Merritt, following a distinguished career in the U.S. Marines, served after World War II as South Carolina legislative counselor. Frederick Sims Lewie (1831–1875), physician and Lexington planter, served in both the state House and Senate. The town of Gilbert Hollow (1878) had its name changed in 1885 to Lewiedale for the prominent family in the area. But the Lewies feuded with railroad officials, who refused to name their new station Lewiedale. Over the years the Lewie family moved from the area, and in 1922 the town's name was again changed to Gilbert (southwest of Lexington between US 1 and I 20).

Lieber

LEE-buh

Lieber College is on the southwest corner of the Horseshoe of the Columbia campus of the University of South Carolina. It was named for the German-born Francis Lieber, internationally renowned professor of political science at Carolina from 1835 to 1857, when he joined the faculty of Columbia University in New York. He is said to have left South Carolina because of strong Unionist sentiments and because he was overlooked for presidency of the college in 1855, but mayhaps a reputed incident when he was professor on duty of a cold winter evening contributed to his leaving: Carolina students took a cow up two flights of stairs to the bell tower of Rutledge College and tied Bossy to the bell rope. The midnight bell tolling and cow bellowing required professorial investigation. On top of old Rutledge was where Lieber first learned that cows will go up stairs but not down, and he outbellowed cow and bell for all the campus to hear his Germanic displeasure: "All of dis for two tousand dollars!" Two of his sons, Hamilton and Norman, also moved to New York in 1857, but his oldest son Oscar, the first state geologist, remained in South Carolina. Lieber Spring in upcountry Abbeville County, a few miles from Calhoun Mill, is named for Oscar Lieber, who worked for some time in the area before the War Between the States. During the war Doctor Lieber asked for a check of casualties of a particularly bloody battle in which two of his sons had fought on opposite sides. "No, sir, your son Norman isn't listed. He must be all right," the Unionist assured him. But then the professor asked for the Confederate casualties. "Oscar Lieber, killed," was the answer.

Lindau

LIN-DOW (rhymes with NOW)

The name is relatively new to South Carolina. Jules Lindau's grandfather emigrated from Alsace-Lorraine to Indiana, and in 1934 Jules Lindau came to Columbia. A chemical engineer, he founded Southern Plastics Company, taught in the School of Engineering at the University of South Carolina, and now serves as a consultant. He and his late wife Bea have been active in community affairs and the Tree of Life Synagogue.

Lobeco
loe-BEE-koe

No, it's not an Indian name; it's a blend. The lowcountry town of Lobeco (US 21, some 15 miles north of Beaufort) was once the seat of a vegetable packinghouse. Two men named Long and Bellamy owned the business. The first two letters of each name plus co for company make up the town's name—though today Long, Bellamy, and the packinghouse all are gone.

Loris
LOE-ris

The Horry town of Loris is north of the county seat, Conway, at US 701 and SC 9. It is reputedly named for a dog owned by the wife of an official of the railroad being built through the area. Some people mispronounce the name LAH-ris.

Louthian
LOW-thi-un (LOW rhymes with now)

Herbert Louthian, Columbia attorney and former Richland County councilman, is a native of upcountry York County, where Louthian families have lived for four generations. The name was originally Lothian (LOE-thi-un), but the first one in the United States had it incorrectly recorded with the extra letter u—Louthian—and he and his descendants have left it that way. Mrs. Herbert Louthian's first name, Rounette (ROO-NET), is also most often mispronounced; so that she has noted, "I'm strange to strangers, first and last."

Lucknow
LUK-NOW

The small community in Lee County was the terminal of a logging railroad from Atkins, Elliott, Wisacky, and Bishopville. The large sawmill in the area was set up to cut virgin longleaf pine. Reputedly, one of the owners, seeing the big stand of beautiful timber for the first time, exclaimed, "We're really in luck now!" Hence the town's name, Lucknow. Or is this an *ex post facto* explanation like the one for Pocataligo?

Lugoff
LOO-GOF (OO as in boot)

Lugoff (US 1, southwest of Camden) is a small town in Kershaw County, named for Russian Count Lugoff, one of the engineers who built the railroad from Richmond to Jacksonville. Lugoff Farm, near the town of Kershaw, is made up of the now combined plantations of Green Hall and Green Hill (the old Whitaker place).

Lynch
LINCH (rhymes with inch)

Thomas Lynch was one of the four South Carolina signers of the Declaration of Independence, July 4, 1776. In the Peedee area's present Florence County, records show Jonah Lynch received a land grant in 1682; there was a Johnson Lynch's Swamp in 1712, and a Lynch's Island in the Santee River in 1737. Lynches River (in early records frequently spelled Linches and termed a creek) originates in North Carolina near the Lancaster County line, meanders from west to east, then southeast to the Peedee River. The river is so curving that, according to Ripley's *Believe It Or Not* and our own eyes, it flows three times under one bridge, the 1250-foot-long bridge on US 1, two miles north of Bethune. Lynches River clay is a profitable export in this arts-and-crafts age. Lynch's Mill, a Lexington County community (US 178 and SC 302), about twenty miles southwest of Columbia, is now named the more erudite Pelion.

McBee
MAK-bi

The unknowing often say mak-BEE, since most Scottish names do not have the accented Mac. The Scottish family is still present in the state, as are also a town, mill, church, and street bearing the name McBee. The town of McBee (US 1 and SC 151) in the North Carolina-bordering county of Chesterfield is named for Colonel "Bunch" McBee, a railroad official. It was he who took over Sydney Park in Columbia for the site of the railroad passenger station. The high cost of the excavation and building resulted in McBee's being fired by the railroad. The Columbia post office is now located there. In 1815 Vardry McBee purchased from Lemuel J. Alston 11,028 acres of Greenville area land. For more than half a century McBee played a generous role in developing Greenville industrially, commercially, educationally, and religiously. Lemuel J. Alston's home Prospect Hill was at the top of the hill on what is now McBee Avenue. McBee Mill on the Reedy River, shown on an 1824 map, is one of the earliest mills in Greenville County. McBee Methodist Church in Conestee (off SC 25) south of Greenville is on the National Register of Historic Places.

McColl
muh-KAWL

The little town of McColl (US 401 and SC 381) is in Marlboro County on the North Carolina border; it is sometimes mispronounced muh-KOLE. As a boy, Duncan Donald McColl (1842–1911) came to South Carolina from Richmond (now Scotland) County, North Carolina, to live with relatives. After service in the Civil War, he practiced law, founded the first bank in Marlboro County, and organized the South Carolina and Pacific Railroad, of which he was president. The first established station on the line was named for him. Eleanor McColl, local historian, is a descendant of Duncan David McColl.

McCreight
muh-KRITE

The three-story McCreight House (1774) in Winnsboro (US 321 and SC 34) north of Columbia is one of the oldest frame houses in Fairfield County. Bobby McCreight was an outstanding athlete at Columbia High School in the late 1930s.

McCullough, McCollough
muh-KUL-uh

The Scotch-Irish name is now found throughout the state. John McCullough settled in Kingstree (US 52 and SC 527) on the Black River in 1735. In the same period James and Andrew McCullough were planters on Hilton Head Island; early maps designate an area there as McCullough's Field. The Rev. John Dewitt McCollough was the architect of St. Stephen's Episcopal Church (1839) in Ridgeway and of Christ Episcopal Church (1820) in Greenville. James McCullough was a lieutenant colonel of the Greenville Regiment, Confederate States of America. In 1941 Fred McCullough, mayor of Greenville, headed the committee that secured the airforce base for that city.

McEachern
muh-KEECH-un

The Scottish pronunciation is muh-KAN, but in South Carolina you have to ask the particular person his preference. Besides muh-KEECH-un and muh-KAN, there is also muh-KA-ha and muh-KUHRN. Clarence Lee McEachern is a Columbia optometrist. Wilbur Washington McEachern is a Greenville banker. The late Furman McEachern was head of state General Services; the legislative parking building on Columbia's Pendleton and Assembly streets has been named for him, pronounced muh-KEECH-un. Daniel Malloy McEachin, Jr., representing Florence County in the state legislature, has perhaps a variant spelling of the same name.

McGehee
muh-GEE (hard G)

The name, still present in the state, is also spelled McGhee and McGee. John and Carr McGehee came from Virginia to the upcountry Greenwood area of old Ninety Six District in 1790. A descendant, possibly a grandson, lawyer John C. McGehee, owned the site of the old pre-Revolutionary Star Fort there, and his home was nearby. Eight miles west of Cambridge he also had a 600-acre tract with a log cabin thereon, which he and his family used for a summer home. His wife called this summer home Greenwood—hence the name of the town that grew up there. (Besides McGehees and Cateechee legends, Greenwood today also has the distinction of having the widest main street in the world, because of its evolution from the Cherokee Path to lots of railroad tracks to the present-day thoroughfare.) In 1840 John C. McGehee moved to northern Florida, where he became a circuit judge and chairman of the Florida Secession Convention. In 1947 his collateral descendant Professor Edward Francis Nolan came to Columbia as a member of the University of South Carolina's Department of English, where he still serves.

McGlamery
muh-GLAM-uh-ri

In the February 1797 term of court in Newberry (upper end of the Dutch Fork, SC 121 and SC 395) William and Hugh McGlamery were each fined $60 for assault and contempt of court (probably fighting in the courtyard). Such is the surname listed in court records and other documents—though the name was actually Montgomery, not McGlamery. The same Billy McGlamery was widely known as one of the "bullies of the fork" and quite a cup-drainer, as evidenced by a poem written about 1900 by John McCreless:

> Billy McGlamery has come to town,
>   To empty cups and glasses!
> He takes the taverns in a line,
>   And drains them as he passes.
>
> He robs the flies of what is their right,
>   And leaves them not a taste, sir!
> I warrant you he stays all night,
>   To see that nothing wastes, sir!

McGuinn
muh-GWIN

Vowel-conscious strangers often say three syllables, muh-GOO-in (oo as in boot). The McGuinn family of Northern Ireland became South Carolinians via Pennsylvania, and North Carolina (Cooper's Gap), finally arriving in Columbia. Jack Francis McGuinn is a trial lawyer. His sister Theresa McGuinn Hicks is a genealogist, one of only twenty-five from the United States and Great Britain invited to lead the week-long Bicentennial Seminar panels held in July 1976 at the National Archives.

McIver
muh-KEE-vuh

Roderick McIver came from Scotland via Ulster (Northern Ireland) to South Carolina in 1756. McIver Street in Cheraw (US 1 and US 52) in Chesterfield County is named for state Chief Justice Henry McIver. Also from Cheraw, Edward McIver (1858–1922) was a lawyer, state senator, and judge. John Edward McIver (1764–1801) of nearby Marlboro County was a lawyer, publisher, planter, and state senator. Petrona McIver, author of *History of Mount Pleasant*, contributed several articles and notes to *Names in South Carolina,* not the least of which was her recipe for Awendaw Cornbread (repeated in this volume, under Awendaw). Other prominent present-day McIvers include Dr. Forde Anderson McIver, pathologist and medical school professor, and Evander Roderick McIver, Jr., lumberman of Conway.

McKeithan
muh-KITH-un

The Scottish-origin McKeithans are still present in Darlington County and surrounding areas. Dugal MacKeithan came to Williamsburg County near Kingstree (US 52 and SC 527) on the Black River about 1730 with the group of settlers led by the Reverend William Screven and his congregation of Dissenters from the Church of England.

McKeown
muh-KOWN

This Scottish-origin family is still present in the state, especially in upcountry Chester (US 321 and SC 121). Pronounced the same way or with a slight third syllable (muh-KOW-uhn), the name is also spelled McCowen.

McLaughlan
muh-GLOK-lin

Revolutionary Colonel McLaughlan, second in command under Colonel Isaac Hayne, was cut to pieces by British Dragoons in July 1781 at the Battle of Ford's Horseshoe Plantation. The plantation of Mrs. Mary Ford was in Colleton County on the east side of Horseshoe Road, which is today called Featherbed Road and is north of SC 64. The McLaughlan name, prevalent throughout the state, is also spelled McLaughlin, McLauchlin, and MacLachlan.

McLean
muh-KLANE

This upcountry Scottish name is also spelled McClain and Mc-Lain. Dutch McLean was long the head of the Episcopal Children's Home in York (US 321 and SC 5). H. B. McLean was postmaster of Blythewood (north of Columbia on US 21). George S. McLean is a Columbia physician.

McLeod
muh-KLOWD

A newcomer's calling our attorney general Dan muh-KLEE-ud and a TV newscast's presenting his name on the screen as "Daniel McCloud" prompted our including this Scottish-origin name from the Peedee section. The name has sometimes been spelled phonetically, McCloud, though the McLeod name is now widespread over the state; in 1982 there were 52 McLeod listings in the Greater Columbia telephone directory. Prominent McLeods in our state have been governor, doctor, lawyer, Methodist minister, and attorney general. Paul ("Dizzy") McLeod was head coach at Furman University, where he had been an outstanding football player. Richard Kirk McLeod is a Sumter lawyer. McLeod Infirmary is a hospital in Florence. McLeod Plantation in Scape O'er Swamp of Lee County was the girlhood home of "Miss Bella," mother of U.S. Senator "Cotton Ed" Smith. The home of Mr. and Mrs. James C. McLeod, Jr., on Cherokee Road in Florence is named Dunvegan for the Scottish McLeod castle on the Isle of Skye, the oldest castle continuously occupied by members of a single family in Europe.

Marjoribanks
MAHRSH-BANGKS

Major John Marjoribanks was the heroic British commander at the Battle of Eutaw Springs (1781)—the last major Revolutionary battle in South Carolina. Marjoribanks was known as "the foe to oppression and the guardian of the unfortunate." He was wounded in the battle, and shortly thereafter he contracted fever, died October 22, 1781, and was buried on Wantoot Plantation, residence of Daniel Ravenel. South Carolinians have a deep respect for a gallant opponent. When the plantation was to be inundated by the waters of Lake Moultrie in the Santee-Cooper project, the remains of Major Marjoribanks were reverently reinterred on the battlefield of Eutaw Springs, with a stone marker nearby.

Manigault
MAN-ni-GOE

This Huguenot family still preserves the French pronunciation of the name. Gabriel Manigault (1704–1781) was a prominent merchant and planter of Colonial Charleston. Manigault Ferry, in Calhoun County across the Santee River below the junction of Congaree and Wateree rivers, was the scene of the Revolutionary battle called Major James Postell's Raid (January 1781). Another Manigault Ferry was in nearby Orangeburg County northwest of Vance (SC 210 and SC 310), south of present Lake Marion. The Manigault name is found throughout South Carolina history. Today Peter Manigault is actively connected with the Charleston *News and Courier*. In Columbia, Manigault Capers is a classic example of a surname being preserved as a given name among descendants. The long-established black Manigault-Hurley Funeral Home in Columbia is pronounced MAN-ni-GAWLT. Manigault Lane is a small black community in Berkeley County, named for prominent black-family residents, who pronounce the name MAN-i-GOTE. The black family names Manago in Florence and Manigo in Aiken are possibly near-phonetic spellings of the name Manigault.

Marley
MAHR-li, MAH-li

As a family name, it is pronounced MAHR-li, but the once-renowned Captain Marley's name has been lost in the pronunciation of South Carolina's monument to him. The outcropping of granite near Newberry (30 miles northwest of Columbia) was originally named for the captain, who was killed by Indians during the Revolution. Over the years Southerners' tendency not to overpronounce the *r* has resulted in the monument's now being officially called Molly's Rock.

Maverick
MAV-uh-RIK

As the old-timers in the Piedmont will tell you about Maverick, "We around Pendleton feel rather possessive of this word." Samuel Augustus Maverick (1802–1870) was one of their boys. A planter and lawyer, he lived at Montpelier, three miles east of Pendleton near the present Greenville highway (now I 85). After moving to Texas, Maverick was a leader in the Texas fight for independence, was mayor of San Antonio, and served in the state legislature. Maverick County on the Mexican border of southwest Texas is named for him. As a rancher he did not follow the custom of branding cattle for identification, so that unmarked cattle came to be called mavericks. The word is now used to refer to an unaffiliated person—an independent, a nonconformist. The newly franchised (1980) Dallas professional basketball team has been named The Mavericks.

Mazyck
muh-ZEEK

The French Huguenot name dates back to Berkeley County land grants: 900 acres in 1764 to William Mazyck and 1,000 acres on Tom's Creek in 1769 to Peter Mazyck. Fair Spring Plantation, now under the waters of Lake Moultrie, was the home of Robert Mazyck. Alexander Mazyck served as state senator, 1848–1865, from St. James Santee. The name has been preserved as a given name. Mazyck Porcher Ravenel was first honor graduate of the Medical College of South Carolina in 1884. William Mazyck Porcher, planter of St. John's Berkeley, was immortalized in Yates Snowden's poem "A Carolina Bourbon," quoted here in part:

His other time he talked and read,
Or else made merry
With many a planter friend to dine,
His health to drink in fine old wine,
Madeira, which thrice crossed the line,
And gold-leaf Sherry

Mazyck's Break is a name given to an open area in Congaree Swamp forest.

Meetze
METS

Also spelled Metz, Metze, and Metts, the name is from the German Mütze. The family is widely known in the state, especially in the Midlands. So far as we know, only the unknowing pronounce it MEETS. The Reverend J. Y. Metze was co-pastor in 1814 at the organization of St. Michael's Lutheran Church in the Dutch Fork near present Irmo on Lake Murray. It's still called the Old Blue Church because the original building (prior to the present one erected in 1921) had a blue ceiling. Henry Adam Meetze (1820–1904), lawyer and tax collector, represented Lexington in the state House and Senate. George Elias Meetze, Lutheran clergyman, has served as chaplain of the state Senate since 1950. Kenneth I. Metz is a Columbia optometrist. His wife June was an active Cub Scout and Brownie den-mother for lots of children in the North Trenholm area of the city. James R. Metts is sheriff of Lexington County.

Mellichamp
MEL-i-SHAMP

Mellisham Gutter on Edisto Island is named for the French Huguenot family, who were early landowners there. A gutter is a narrow saltwater drain that interlaces the marshes, usually dry at low tide. Another local name given by the Sea Island blacks is Shingle Creek, derived from the fact that the stream could just barely float a shingle at low tide. One of William Gilmore Simms's Revolutionary War novels bears the title *Mellichampe* (1836). Joseph Hinson Mellichamp (1829–1903) practiced medicine at Bluffton (SC 46) in southern Beaufort County. Actively pursuing an avocation of botany, he contributed greatly to the knowledge of lowcountry flora. A medicinal plant of the milkweed family, Mellichampia, is named for him. "Miss Nell" Mellichamp taught piano on Shandon's Queen Street to many a Columbia child from the 1930s until she died. David St. Claire Mellichamp, native of Longtown in Fairfield County, practiced law in Columbia in the years after 1940.

Mesopotamia
MES-suh-puh-TAME-i-uh

Established before 1800, Mesopotamia Methodist Church is located in upcountry Cherokee County between the Pacolet and Broad rivers. It takes its name from the ancient Greek word for the area between the Euphrates and Tigris Rivers, literally meaning "between the rivers."

Michaux, Micheaux, Michau, Mishoe
mi-SHOE, mi-SHOO
(long o in SHOE; OO as in boot in SHOO)

The present name is often written Mishoe or Misho and sometimes pronounced mi-SHOO (OO as in boot). The original French Huguenot, Micheaux, settled at Jamestown (US 17A and SC 41) in Berkeley County and later moved across the river at Lenud's Ferry and settled along the Santee River. Of the early French settlers there (including also the Lequeux and Peronneau families), only the Mishoe family is still present in the area. Their name is pronounced mi-SHOE, but in Horry County some Mishoe families pronounce their name mi-SHOO. The French botanist André Michaux (1746–1802) brought the first camellias to America in 1787 and planted them at Middleton Place on the Ashley River. Mashawville (pronounced mi-SHOE-vul), four miles from Walterboro on the Charleston Road, was named for Henry Michaux, who lived there in 1755. His widow married Dr. James Reid, and their daughter married a Pringle. The little community is now called Pringle Bend, although on the Colleton County map Mashawville School House still bears the misspelled name. State senators have included Paul Michau, representing All Saints, 1804–1810, and the two brothers Leonard Galloway Mishoe and William Frank Mishoe, representing Williamsburg County in the 1950s and 1960s respectively. The family plantation at Michaux's Point is now part of Hobcaw Barony, in the southern part of Waccamaw Neck in Georgetown County.

Mimnaugh
MIM-NAW

Mimnaugh Bottom is an alley off the 1400 block of Huger Street in downtown Columbia near the law enforcement complex. It was named for the family that owned much land in the area in the 1920s. Mimnaugh Department Store flourished on Columbia's Main Street before the 1929 crash. Its owner was a demanding taskmaster. One of his customers remembers his summoning a clerk with stomping foot and clapping hands: "When Mimnaugh says *Come*, come a-running!" And when the financial crash came, he summed up his plight just as tersely: "When Mimnaugh's through, he's through!" The now destroyed Mimnaugh House on Gervais Street at Henderson (now the site of the Carolina Town House Motel) was headquarters for General William T. Sherman (February 1865) and one of the few buildings he left unmatched.

Modoc
MOE-DOK

Apparently it was during the fierce Modoc Indian war in Oregon that railroad agents, seeking rights-of-way in present McCormick County, felt they were being "scalped" by property owners. The railroad officials therefore imported from the Far West the Indian name Modoc for the station on their victimized line. Modoc is near Clark's Hill Reservoir (US 221 and SC 23), west of Edge-field.

Moise
moe-EEZ

Moise Drive in Sumter (US 76 and US 15) east of Columbia passes through Moise family land. It is possibly named for General E. Warren Moise, as was Sumter's Warren Street. Marion Moise (1855–1910), lawyer and banker, and his son David De-Leon Moise (1880–1931) were both state senators from Sumter. Harold Moise (b. 1897) has written a history of the Moise family.

Monticello
MON-ti-SEL-uh

Monticello Road is the local name for SC 215 leading north from Columbia to the little village of Monticello in Fairfield County. On the Mills Atlas of 1820 it's termed "the road to Chester Court House." Although the name is derived from Thomas Jefferson's home (pronounced MON-ti-CHEL-oe from the Italian word meaning low hill), the name of our road has the S rather than the CH sound. During Jefferson's presidency, in 1802, the Jefferson-Monticello Society was created by act of the state legislature for the purpose of establishing a school or academy in the village of Monticello. The Jefferson-Monticello Academy became the Zealy Academy for Girls during the Civil War, and afterwards the Monticello Public School. In early years the village had great expectations for growth. Streets were laid out and lots were sold by William J. Alston, president of the society in 1837. Earlier commissioners of the village were William Cato, Benjamin May, Joshua Durham, and Phillip Pearson. Today there are only a couple dozen residences there.

Montmorenci
MONT-muh-REN-si

The town of Montmorenci (US 78, about six miles southeast of Aiken) was named by a landowner who noted that the beauty of the area reminded him of the Vale of Montmorency in France. Legend has it that the town was earlier named Pole Cat. Old-timers in the community resented the change to the fancier title until they were pacified by the dubious explanation that "Montmorenci" is "French" for Pole Cat.

Moragné
muh-RIE-ni

The French Huguenot family settled in New Bordeaux (1765) along the Savannah River in old Abbeville District. Mary E. Moragné wrote the novel *The British Partizan* (1838) and kept a journal (1836–1842) of her life in the Huguenot community, published in 1951 by The University of South Carolina Press as *The Neglected Thread*. The Confederate War edition of *The British Partizan* was published in 1864 and sold to Confederate soldiers for 75 cents a copy. There is no record of how much Yankee soldiers paid for a copy. The Moragné name is still present in Abbeville and McCormick counties.

Motte
MOT (rhymes with hot)

The Calhoun County town of Fort Motte (SC 419, off US 601 near the junction of Congaree and Wateree rivers) is really not a fort. The designation resulted from a Revolutionary battle at the home of Colonel and Mrs. (Rebecca Brewton) Isaac Motte. In 1781 the Colonel was off in the war, and his home had been occupied by the British to be used for ammunition storage. With permission and encouragement from Mrs. Motte, General Francis Marion's men shot flaming arrows into the house so that the fear of wholesale explosion drove the British outside to defeat. For the Revolutionary Bicentennial Mrs. Nell Peterkin Reid, avid local historian of nearby Oakland Plantation, directed her grandchildren and their friends in the re-enactment of the Battle of Fort Motte, from which they made an excellent movie. Also near Fort Motte is Lang Syne Plantation, home of Julia Mood Peterkin, Pulitzer Prize-winning author of *Scarlet Sister Mary* (1928), one of her several color-titled books (others are *Green Thursday* and *Black April*). Terry L. Motte served as a Baptist minister in West Columbia in the early 1980s.

Moultrie

MOOL-tri (OO as in boot)

Next to Huger, Moultrie is probably the South Carolina name most frequently butchered by the talking media: the weathermen give the water level of Lake MOLE-tri and the sportscasters tell us how the fish are biting at Lake MOLE-tri. Once when one of them was called on it, he explained, "Yes, ma'am, I know it's MOOL-tri, but don't you think MOLE-tri sounds better?" For that, the General might well have run him through (see Kinloch for an account of Moultrie's dueling). General William Moultrie (1730–1805), as a Revolutionary colonel, repulsed the British at the Battle of Sullivan's Island in 1776. The Fort was made of palmetto logs; their ability to absorb the British cannon balls and Sergeant William Jasper's heroic restoring of the fallen flag are stories often associated with the battle. Moultrie published his *Memoirs of the American Revolution* in 1802. He served on the Legislative Council, in the state Senate, and twice as governor. His Scottish family name is now given to the fort he defended, the lake formed by water diverted from Lake Marion to the Cooper River in Berkeley County, and the town of Moultrieville in Charleston County. The family name still survives and is still pronounced MOOL-tri. (However, in Georgia the accepted pronunciation for the town of Moultrie is now MOLE-tri.)

Mouzon

moo-ZON (OO as in boot)

Mouzon's Map (1775) was the first accurate map of North and South Carolina. Captain Henry Mouzon, French Huguenot of Williamsburg County (lowcountry area of Kingstree, US 52 and SC 527), was a civil engineer, cartographer, planter, and soldier. He served under Francis Marion in the Revolution and was severely wounded at the Battle of Black Mingo. His plantation home and fourteen buildings on the east side of Pudding Swamp near Black River were burned by British Colonel Banastre Tarleton. The town of Mouzon in Williamsburg County is named for him. Harold Alwyn Mouzon (born 1893 in Bamberg) was a Charleston lawyer with special interest in maritime history.

Murrell

MUH-rul

Murrells Inlet, a popular Grand Strand resort with some of the best seafood eating in the area, derives its name from John Morrall, who settled there about 1815. Modern mapmakers spell the name Murrell's and Murrells Inlet, but the U.S. Board of Geographical Names, preferring accuracy, has changed the spelling to Morrall's Inlet. Nevertheless, the community and the post office have remained Murrells Inlet, which is still the name used by the homefolks and people throughout the state. John Fripp Morrell, Beaufort merchant and local historian, is a descendant of the first John and pronounces his name muh-RAL.

Neeses

NEE-sez (like nieces)

Neeses (US 321 and SC 4) is about 40 miles south of Columbia in Orangeburg County. It was named in 1890 for J. W. Neese, a landowner there.

Nesmith
NEE-SMITH

The town of Nesmith (road 24) on Black Mingo Creek in Williamsburg County was settled in 1725. It was named for early settler John Nesmith, who was born in Northern Ireland in 1670 and died in his new lowcountry homeland in 1750. The Nesmith post office was established in 1907 with R. J. Nesmith as postmaster. Among the other talents of Harold Nesmith, a present descendant, was some mighty good bird hunting in earlier days; we still remember his partridges and hominy for breakfast.

Neuffer
NIFE-uh

The unknowing sometimes pronounce it NOO-fuhr, perhaps under the impression that it's a Huguenot name. In fact it's of German origin. The German pronunciation would be NOI-fuhr, but less mouth-twisting Southern speech now prefers NIFE-uh (one who knifes). In 1775 Herman Neuffer, a Charleston merchant on King Street, drove a wagonload of rifles to the upcountry with a letter from Arthur Middleton to William Drayton directing that Neuffer be supplied with circular letters and other papers to assist him in bringing the backcountry settlers over to the patriots' cause. Prior to the War Between the States, Charles Neuffer was sheriff of Richland County and owner-resident of the house at Gervais and Sumter streets where the Bankers Trust Building, topped by the Summit Club, now stands. (If Sherman just hadn't burned those property records, we might have reached the Summit.) Dr. Gottlob Augustus Neuffer (1861–1935), born in Orangeburg, practiced medicine in Abbeville, founded a savings and loan association and a drug store, served in the state legislature, and bottled Knifer's Tonic—for over 75 years a popular deterrent to colds, coughs, and sore throats. Neuffer's Classical Academy in Columbia and Neuffer's School in Bennettsville in the Peedee area were named for the doctor's brother, Claude Victor Neuffer, a teacher who was widely known in the state. Students at the Columbia academy included the late A. C. (Zan) Heyward, James

McIntosh, Julian Hook, Jim McCoy, and Pierre F. LaBorde, who in later years titled it Neuffer's Reform School and delighted in calling the co-author of this book "the Warden's nephew." Lt. Judy Neuffer of Ohio, the first woman navy pilot to fly through the eye of a hurricane, has given in and accepts the pronunciation NOO-fuhr. But in South Carolina even the first-graders learn it's NIFE-uh, as teacher Sarah Neuffer's young student wrote in his December letter: "Dear Santa Claus, Please bring me a boy-scout neuf."

Ninety Six
NINE-ti SIKS

The natives are mighty particular about there not being a hyphen in their town's name, so it's included here for the misspellers, rather than the mispronouncers. Ninety Six (SC 34 and SC 246) in old Abbeville District is east of the city of Greenwood in Greenwood County. It was the site of a pre-Revolutionary garrison called the Star Fort. Its name derives from the fact that the fort was 96 miles down the Cherokee Path from Keowee, headquarters of the Cherokee Indians in Oconee County. (The old town of Keowee is now under water, courtesy of the Duke Power Plant; the present town of Keowee is nearby on US 123.) The story that the town of Ninety Six and all the creeks along the path were named by the fast-riding Indian maid Cateechee in the 1760 Indian War is disproved by earlier maps.

Nitrolee
NIE-TROE-LEE

In 1917 W. S. Lee came to the upcountry area around Chester (US 321 and SC 72) with a machine which was supposed to glean nitrogen from the air. About the same time a power plant was established and a town grew up there. Although the contraption failed in its assignment, the town (contiguous with Great Falls) was named Nitrolee to commemorate Mr. Lee and his unsuccessful nitrogen machine.

Notlee
NOT-LEE

Like Wasbee, this Charleston street name may appear to have an Indian origin, but it actually evolved quite differently. It was one of several pairs of streets in the city with identical names. In this case, there were two Lee streets. To eliminate confusion city council declared this one NOT-LEE Street.

Oconee
oe-KONE-ee

The Indian name possibly refers to the mythical Cherokee snake dragon, or it may mean "the water eyes of the hills." Oconee is South Carolina's northwesternmost county, which was part of old Pendleton District. The county's oldest building, Oconee Station, is northwest of Walhalla. It was a military outpost used both before and after the Revolution to protect the people from hostile Indians. In 1800 Oconee Station was used as a trading post.

okra
OE-kruh

One of the state's abundant crops, this spiney-podded staple ingredient of the revered okra soup has been eulogized in Yates Snowden's poem, " 'Okrantomatis' ":

> When days are dark and trouble lowers,
> And flowers, leaves and spirits droop,
> What force revivifies our powers?
> That panacea, OKRA SOUP.

Related names include Okra Baptist Church near Springfield (SC 4 and SC 39) in Orangeburg County and the Okra Strut, an annual festival in Lexington County. Every October since 1974 the Irmo–Lake Murray Women's Club has sponsored the Okra Strut as a fund-raiser for the Lexington County Branch Library and other civic projects. The carnival-like affair held at Seven Oaks Recreation Center is very popular even for those who don't like okra for various reasons; not the least of these reasons—boiled okra's slimy quality—was cited by Allan Young, the kindly black Cedar Creek resident, when he proclaimed: "I don't put nothing in my mouth over which I don't have no control."

Oliphant
AH-li-funt

For over sixty years William Gilmore Simms's *History of South Carolina* has been a textbook of the state public schools, frequently revised by Simms's granddaughter and co-editor of his letters, Mary Chevillette Simms Oliphant. Raised at the family plantation, Woodlands, now in Bamberg County, Mrs. Oliphant has long lived in Greenville at 107 James Street, the oldest home (built about 1810) in the county. Both homes are on the National Register of Historic Places. David Olyphant (1720–1805) came to South Carolina in 1746 from Scotland, where he had supported the Stuart kings. In Charleston he was a physician and planter. During the Revolution he was director general of hospitals in the Southern Department, a member of the first and second Provincial Congresses and of the Legislative Council; later he was a representative and then a senator from St. George, Dorchester. Jim Oliphant, columnist of the Spartanburg *Herald*, has over the years sent *Names in South Carolina* delightful notes on place names, including Fingerville, Sugar Tit, and Kegtown.

Ora
OH-ruh

The village of Ora (1885) in Laurens County is near the intersection of US 221 and SC 308. Previously this settlement and voting precinct on the Laurens to Spartanburg road had been called Scuffletown. When the railroad was being built through the area, the surveyor Tyler McDonald was instructed to consult residents for a shorter and more pleasant name. In love with a local lass Leora Hunter (whom he later married), McDonald reputedly consulted only his heart: omitting the first syllable of Leora's name, he submitted the name Ora for the railroad station and post office.

Oswego
os-WEE-goe

Though variously called OS-wee-goe, os-WAE-goe, and even OE-SWAE-goe by outsiders, the natives of the quiet little Sumter County village prefer os-WEE-goe. On US 401, north of Sumter, the town was named for Oswego, New York, hometown of one of the officials of the railroad being built through the area. In the 1890s the new Charleston, Sumter and Northern Railroad station made the town important. But highways and trucks have changed shipping ways, and today Oswego is just another zip code, 29121 via Sumter.

Ouzts
OOTS (rhymes with boots)

The Ouzts family of German origin is one of the largest family groups in Greenwood County. Deidrich Utz came to Charleston in 1766, moved on to Newberry, then to the section northwest of Edgefield called the Dutch Settlement. According to the recorded will of his son Peter, by then the family name had become Ouzts. By 1880 there were 940 descendants of Deidrich Utz; his son Peter had eleven sons and one daughter. Among our political sobriquets such as "Pitchfork Ben" Tillman and "Cotton Ed" Smith was the upcountry's "Dago" Ouzts, from the initials of Daniel Andrew Gaines Ouzts (1863–1946), who served in the state House and Senate from Greenwood County. William C. Ouzts, attorney, has long served as city councilman of Columbia.

Pacolet
PAK-uh-let

It has variously been suggested that the place name derives from
an early settler, a character in a French ballad, a French word
meaning swift runner, or an Indian word meaning running horse.
Pacolet Station, Pacolet Park, Central Pacolet, and Pacolet Mills
are east of upcountry Spartanburg in the area around US 176 and
SC 150. Pacolet Mills was once called Trough Shoals. Pacolet
Mineral Spring was the first of several springs in the county to
receive widespread recognition as a health spa. In the 1790s it was
a stagecoach stop on the route from Yorkville (present York, US
321 and SC 49) to Spartanburg. In 1825 it was known as Poole's
Springs, and in 1855 R. C. Poole operated a hotel there for 40 to
50 boarders in "plain decent country style."

Palmer
PAH-muh, PAM-muh

Palmer Street in Winnsboro is named for Edward Gendron
Palmer, first of the lowcountry planters to settle in the Ridgeway
section (US 21 and SC 34) of Fairfield County, north of Columbia. He built two handsome plantation homes there: Valencia
(1834), where he lived, and Cedar Tree (1853) for his son Dr.
John Davis Palmer. Six Palmers in the eighteenth and nineteenth
centuries were senators from the Ridgeway area (sometimes
called St. Stephens Parish from the lowcountry origin of its prominent citizens). Most of the Palmers from this area and the lowcountry preserve the Santee River pronunciation PAM-muh. In
upcountry Union the Palmers answer to the more usual PAH-muh.

Parris
PA-ris (short A, short i)

Because of its French connection (it was the location of the
doomed 1562 settlement of Jean Ribaut and his fellow Huguenots), Parris Island is more often misspelled with one *r* than it is

mispronounced. In Beaufort County in the fork between the Beaufort and Broad rivers, off the tip of Port Royal Island and across a creek, Parris Island is named for Colonel Alexander Parris, colonial treasurer of South Carolina. The island is now a U.S. Marine Base.

Paslay

PAZE-li (like paisley)

Pasley Place in upcountry Laurens County near Mountville (SC 72, south of Clinton) was built in 1785 by Captain Paslay. It is one of the oldest homes in the county and is now being renovated by Calhoun Graham, great-great-grandson of the original owner. Robert B. Paslay, Spartanburg attorney, is also a great-great-grandson of Captain Paslay. There is a street in Sumter called Paisley Park.

Paquereaux

PAK-uh-ROE

This French Huguenot name has been given the phonetic spelling Packerow by some of the family.

Peay

PEE, PAE (like pea and pay)

Both pronunciations are used in the state, so you'll have to check with the individual as to which one he prefers. The Peays were one of the largest planter families of antebellum days in Fairfield County (north of Columbia on US 21) near Ridgeway. Nicholas Adamson Peay (1811–1857), a cotton planter, served in the state Senate from Fairfield County. Melrose, the Peay family home in the old Longtown section, was burned by General Sherman in 1865. Farther north, Peay's Ferry was on the Wateree River south of Liberty Hill (SC 97 and 522). General Sherman crossed the river at Peay's Ferry and camped thereby for nine days of plundering.

Peden

PADE-uhn (rhymes with maiden)

Pronunciations PEED-un and PED-un are sometimes heard but not acceptable to those who bear the name. John Peden came to America in the early 1700s. He was founder of the Scottish Covenanter family among the early settlers in the Fairview section of upcountry Greenville County. Fairview Presbyterian Church, the mother of Presbyterians in the county, is closely associated with Pedens. Their annual family reunion is held there. In the church cemetery a marble monument to John and Mary Peden bears on one side the coat of arms of South Carolina and the Scotch thistle paired with the Irish shamrock. Peggy and John Peden are listed in pre-Revolutionary records as residents of the upcounty Chester County area. Peden's Bridge Road off SC 97 was the location of an antebellum Mobley family mansion with glass set in the square columns—a mark of the Mobleys wherever they lived. Peden McLeod, of lowcountry Walterboro (US 15 and US 17A) is a recently elected state Senator.

Peedee

PEE-DEE

In records the word is variously spelled Pedee, PeeDee, and Peedee. The late A. S. Salley, state historian for over 40 years, was firmly convinced it should be Peedee; Cook's and Mouzon's maps also used Peedee. Though historian Robert Duncan Bass preferred Pedee, he opposed PeeDee and compromised with his publishers so that he also used Peedee. Here we side with the experts—newspaper reporters to the contrary—though we are aware that since the Indian language was not written the spelling of Peedee is a matter of choice. The Peedee River and its surrounding Peedee section (Florence, being its chief city) run from the North Carolina line southeast to the coast. In colonial grants the presently named Little Peedee River—the boundary line between Marion and Horry counties, east of the Peedee—was Cypress River. Peedee is an Indian word meaning wading, shallow, or crossing place —all qualities of this river. The Peedee Indians were a small tribe of Sioux who dwelled between the Cheraws and the Winyaws. There is little truth to the story that an early trader named Patrick Daley, as he made his way up the river valley, carved his initials, P.D., on trees along the trail so that the river and area were called Peedee.

Pegues
puh-GEEZ

Descendants of Revolutionary Captain Claudius Pegues still occupy the family's original land grant in Marlboro County in the Peedee area. Christopher Butler Pegues (1789–1846), Cheraw planter, served in the state House and Senate. The family name is prevalent in Chesterfield County around Cheraw, in Marlboro County, and in lowcountry Summerville in Dorchester County.

Pelham
PEL-um

The upcountry community of Pelham (SC 14, off I 85) is on the Enoree River between Greenville and Spartanburg. In 1820 it was Pelham Mill, but the mill and company store burned many years ago. It may be the same store area that today has a different unofficial name: a news reporter, trying to pinpoint the location of a tornado, asked an elderly resident, "What's this place called, ma'am?" She answered, "It's the road to Pelham." But her little charge pulled on her skirt to interrupt, "Ah, Granny, everybody knows it's Sugar Tit." The story is that after a day in the mill and a noisy supper in the midst of his large family, the man of the house retreated to the general store for a bit of calm and several cups of cheer. And when his brood would ask, "Where's Daddy?" Momma would sigh, "Oh, he's gone to get his Sugar Tit." Hence the store was called Sugar Tit, and the area nearby still bears the name. (For the unknowing, a sugar tit for a baby is a homemade pacifier of a tightly tied nipple-shaped wad of cloth dipped in sugar water.)

Pelion
PEEL-yun

Pelion (US 178 and SC 302) of the Midlands is in Lexington County about twenty miles southwest of Columbia. Formerly named Lynch's Mill, the town derives its present name from the Greek myth in which giants attempted to heap Mount Ossa on Mount Pelion to reach heaven. Perhaps a resident gave the town its erudite name because he considered his Pelion "right next to heaven."

Pendarvis
pen-DAHR-vis

The Pendarvis families are still prevalent in the Orangeburg area, where Joseph Pendarvis of Charleston had early land grants. Records reveal that the initial Joseph Pendarvis and his wife Elizabeth came to Carolina with the first English expedition in 1670.

Peronneau
PEH-ruh-NOE

Henry Peronneau came with his wife Desire from La Rochelle, France, to the Carolina Province in 1687. The family settled with other French Huguenots on Santee River near Lenud's Ferry. William Henry Peronneau was a captain in the First Regiment, South Carolina Regular Artillery, Confederate States of America. He commanded a battery in Fort Sumter at the memorable repulse of the federal fleet in April 1863. After the war he was president of the Washington Light Infantry, which published a memorial to him at his passing in 1874.

Petigru, Pettigrew

PET-ti-GROO (OO as in boot)

The original law-school building of Columbia's University of South Carolina campus was named for the prominent Unionist lawyer, James Louis Petigru (1789–1863). Born in upcountry old Abbeville District as a Pettigrew, he changed his name to give it a French flavor; his mother was a Huguenot Gibert. Petigru actively opposed South Carolina's proposed secession, saying, "They've gone mad. South Carolina is too small to be a republic and too large to be a lunatic asylum." Petigru Street, in northeast Columbia and Forest Acres, is named for him. Confederate General James Johnson Pettigrew chose to keep the Scottish spelling of his name. Bonnie Shade, one of only two antebellum homes in Florence, was built by James E. Pettigrew before 1856. On Cherokee Road, it is now the home of Mr. and Mrs. Mark W. Buyck, Jr.

Petit, Pettit

puh-TEE, PET-it

It's another name for the pronunciation of which you'll have to consult the owner, since some have given up the original French for the near-phonetic anglicized pronunciation: e.g., the Bill Pettit family in Columbia answers to PET-it. The first contingent of the Petit-Guerard colony landed at Oyster Point (Charleston) in April 1680, following petitions of Rene Petit and Jacob Guerard. The Petit and Pettit families are now found throughout the state: e.g., Howard Gordon Pettit, Jr., Walhalla lawyer; Dr. Edward LeRoy Petit, Greenwood dentist; Sam Layton Pettit, Spartanburg civil engineer; Louise Pettit, Columbia portrait painter; and James Percival Petit, author of *Freedom's Four Square Miles* (1964) on the history of Charleston Harbor.

Peyre
PEH-uh

This French Huguenot name is almost extinct as a family name
in the state, but it is preserved in given names of descendants:
e.g., Peyre Thomas and Peyre Scurry. John Peyre (1750–1807),
planter of Laurel Hill Plantation on the Cooper River, represented
St. Stephen's in the state House and Senate. At the request of
the Confederate Surgeon General, Dr. Francis Peyre Porcher
wrote *Resources of Southern Fields and Forests* describing foods,
medicines, and necessities of life that could be gathered in the
wild. He also taught at the state medical college, edited the
Charleston Medical Review, and was vice-president of the American Medical Association. Dr. John Peyre Thomas' Mount Hope
Plantation was built in the 1830s in Fairfield County, southeast of
Winnsboro near Ridgeway; it is still owned by the Thomas family.
His son Captain John Peyre Thomas led Columbia's Arsenal
Academy cadets against Stoneman's Raiders at Williamston on
May 1, 1865—the last Civil War engagement east of the Missis-
sippi.

Pigate
PIE-gut

This French Huguenot family lives in the Florence–Darlington
area of the Peedee. The name has also been spelled Piggott and
Pigat (pronounced PIG-ut).

pilau
PUHR-LOE, pi-LOE

Though dictionaries identify pilau as a Persian dish, with all man-
ner of pronunciations, South Carolinians have their own mixtures
and pronunciations for this all-in-one rice-meat dish. Making a
pilau was an especially helpful way to use leftovers or stretch the
meat dish during Reconstruction and the Great Depression. A

very tasty non-tomato concoction is Hampton Plantation Shrimp Pilau, contributed by Harriott Horry Rutledge to the Charleston Junior League's longtime popular cookbook, *Charleston Receipts* (translated *Recipes* for Carolinians not of the "old school").

Pinopolis
pie-NOP-uh-lis

The quiet little community of Pinopolis in Berkeley County is three miles northwest of Moncks Corner on a peninsula jutting into Lake Moultrie. This "city of the pines," named by resident F. A. Porcher in the 1820s, began as a summer retreat and refuge from malaria for plantation families in the area. Only nine of the old homes remained some fifteen years ago when new houses began to appear in several subdivisions.

Pocataligo
POKE-uh-TAL-li-goe

Sometimes spelled Pocotaligo, Pocataligo (US 17 off I 95) is a town in lowcountry Jasper County, south of the Combahee River. The word, from the Yemassee Indians, means gathering place. The name in no way has its origin in the oft-repeated story of the man coping with his balking mule before a group of wits hunkered down in front of the general store. Among their many reported words of advice were, "Poke his tail, he go." The mule owner did; the mule moved on; and ever since then the place has been called Pocataligo. That's what's called an ex post facto explanation. And it's not true, even when the story makes it slow turtles crossing the road. Some people believe that a shortened form of Pocataligo is evident in Sumter County in Pocalla Swamp, three miles south of Sumter on US 15, where there are also Pocalla Road and Pocalla Tourist Court (pronounced poe-KAL-luh).

Poco Sabo
POE-KOE   SAH-BOE

Poco Sabo in Colleton County on the lowcountry Ashepoo River was the plantation home of Landgrave Edmund Bellinger, who is buried there.

Pomaria
POE-MEH-ri-uh

Pomaria (US 176 off I 26) is in the Dutch Fork east of Newberry. Though the name is often mispronounced POE-MER-ri, its origin has nothing to do with an indigent "Po' Mary" having lived there. From 1840 to 1878 William Summer operated a business titled Pomaria (from the Latin word for orchards or fruit gardens), which was one of the largest and most complete nurseries in the South. He also started Pomaria Stock Farm, improving cattle, swine, and sheep. Some members of the Shealy family claim that their forebear named the town Pomaria for his European home in Pomerania (now part of Poland).

Pompion
PUNGK-in

Pompion, said to be derived from a French word meaning pumpkin, is pronounced PUNGK-in by the Berkeley County folk where Pompion Hill Chapel overlooks the East Branch of the Cooper River from a high bluff. The first church there, serving Huguenot families turned Anglican, was built in 1703; the present structure dates from 1766. Nearby Pompion Hill Plantation was the home of the Reverend Thomas Hasell, who came from England to serve the church in 1709.

Porcher

pohr-SHAE

To our knowledge only the truly unknowing think Porcher is phonetically pronounced like the Southerner who relaxes in a rocking chair on the front piazza and watches the world go by. This Huguenot family is one of the few that have retained both the French pronunciation and the French spelling of their name. The Porchers were such a large family in the antebellum era that they were called "a mighty nation." They owned several plantations in lowcountry Berkeley County—Mexico, Peru, Ophir, Sarazins, and Walworth—and large landholdings in other counties. In 1751 Isaac Porcher owned 200 acres in lower Richland County. Porcher Avenue in Eutawville (SC 6 and SC 453, on present Lake Marion) is named for family landowners there. Porcher's Bluff, seven miles from Mount Pleasant near Dewee's Island, has been the mecca for five generations of homing Porchers. When Isaac and Percival Porcher of St. John's Berkeley died in the early 1930s, the last South Carolinians of "pure Huguenot descent" passed away. But there is still a host of people and places in these parts that bear the name.

Powe

POE

Powe Street in Cheraw (US 1 and US 52) is named for General Erasmus Powe. At one time the far side of the next street, Boundary, was called Powe Town since the family plantations (now called Enfield and Hartzell House) were located there. Boxwood Hall and Heartease, also in Cheraw, were homes built by Dr. Thomas H. Powe.

Poyas

PIE-yus (like pious)

It's another French Huguenot name, the pronunciation of which has been Carolinized. The John E. Poyas house, 69 Meeting Street in Charleston, was built about 1796 and is now the home of Mr. and Mrs. C. N. Bayless. One of the present descendants, who asks to be nameless, bears Poyas as a middle name and comments, "Since I have neither the property nor the pride of my forebears, appropriately my middle name should be pronounced POE-ASS!"

Prevost
pruh-VOE

Prevost ladies of DAR membership might also be eligible for DAT or DAB (Daughters of American Tories or British) if there were such organizations. Prevost's Raid (March–May 1779) is the name given to expeditions by British Major General Augustine Prevost in the Carolina lowcountry between the Savannah River and Charleston; Prevost's raids were as notorious as General William T. Sherman's later march and for similar reasons, though in general Prevost found plundering Carolinians' property more profitable than burning it. Cuthbert B. Prevost, formerly of Columbia, now lives in Georgetown. His wife Charlotte Kaminski Prevost, a direct descendant of George Pawley, is co-author with Effie Leland Wilder of *Pawley's Island . . . A Living Legend* (1972).

Prioleau
PRAE-LOE (rhymes with halo)

This Huguenot name is still present in the state, but the pronunciation is only semi-French. After the destruction of his French Protestant Church of Pons, France, in 1687, Pastor Elias Prioleau with many of his congregation came to Charleston, where he became pastor of the French Church. Philip Prioleau served as librarian of the Charleston Library Society, 1787–1790. The John Cordes Prioleau House at 68 Meeting Street in Charleston was built about 1816. Praylow, a family name in the upcountry, is apparently a phonetic spelling of the same name, as perhaps is the given name of Pralo Wood of Tigerville, who served 28 years as deputy sheriff of Greenville County.

Pugh

PUE (rhymes with few)

The name is spelled Pugh, Pou, and Pough—all pronounced PUE. Alice Pugh, a Virginia native, was a teacher at Columbia's old Shandon School in the 1930s. Attorney Pou Taylor, was Richland County solicitor. Olin Sharpe Pugh, native of Dutch Fork, Newberry, is a professor in the School of Business Administration at the University of South Carolina, Columbia campus. Mrs. Carolyn Pough Sutton, secretary in the English Department of the University of South Carolina, is from the black Pough family of the town of Neeses (US 321 and SC 4) in Orangeburg County.

Pulaski

pue-LAS-ki, puh-LAS-ki

One of Columbia's north-south running streets west of Assembly Street is named for General Casimir Pulaski, the Polish officer who fought for the colonists in the Revolution and died in the defense of the South Carolina and Georgia lowcountry in 1779. In the initial plan for Columbia (1786) as the capital city, all streets running north and south were named for Revolutionary generals. (Thus we also have such streets as Huger, Lincoln, Sumter, Marion, Bull and Pickens.) Only the unknowing give the general the broad A, puh-LAH-ski.

Purrysburg

PUE-riz-BUHRG, PUEZ-BUHRG

The area on the east bank of the Savannah River between Day's Creek and King Creek, not far upstream from the city of Savannah, was settled about 1732 by Swiss immigrants led by Colonel Jean Pierre Pury, Director General of the French East India Company. The journal of the Commons House of Assembly (April 20, 1751) refers to "the high road to Purrys Burgh." A 1791 land grant to John M. Iriel uses the present spelling in locating his land "two or three miles above Purrysburg Township."

Quinine
KWIE-NINE, KWIN-NINE

Some people pronounce the antimalarial drug kwi-NEEN, but you will be taken for a stranger if you pronounce Quinine Hill that way. Quinine Hill was long the name given to lands north of the present intersection of Forest Drive and Beltline Boulevard in greater Columbia's northeast section. The mineral spring there was supposedly good for combatting malaria. Perhaps more to the point, the high land provided a summer retreat from the mosquitoes in the river valley of the town. More recently Quinine Hill was the country estate of the late Senator James H. Hammond, attorney and delightful raconteur. It is now a residential area.

Rantowles
RAN-TOLEZ (second syllable rhymes with moles)

Rantowles Bridge was south of the Ashley River in Charleston County, corresponding to US 17 over Rantowles Creek today. John Rutledge (president and governor of the state, 1776–1782) had his Stono Plantation near the bridge, close by the scene of a Revolutionary battle. Two undocumented stories suggest the origin of the name. At one time a Mr. Wilkie operated a ferry there; hence he *ran tolls,* and the name has been corrupted (or improved?) to Rantowles. An alternative explanation has it that the Ravenels and the Towles were early landowners in the area, and the name of the community was originally a blend of those two names: Ravtowles; but the handwritten v was misread as an n, resulting in Rantowles—as the name has been from Revolutionary times.

Raoul
ROWL (rhymes with OWL)

The French name was originally Raoul de Champmanoir. The first of the family here was exiled by Napoleon and came to South

Carolina in 1812; he married Caroline Theus Thomson of St.
Matthews Parish (now Calhoun County, south of Columbia), and
anglicized his name to John Louis Raoul. A descendant, Thomas
J. Goodwin, was mayor of Columbia when General Sherman visited in 1865.

Ravenel
RAV-uh-NEL

The lowcountry town of Ravenel (SC 165, just south of US 17)
is named for the French Huguenot family. Ravenel, as a place
name, is widespread, with a Ravenel Precinct in northwest Oconee
County and Ravenel Street in Columbia's residential Shandon.
St. John's Berkeley was represented in the state Senate (1810–
1822) by Ravenel brothers Stephen and Daniel James. More recently Charles ("Pug") Ravenel was Democratic nominee for
Governor (1974), but disqualified on the residential requirement;
Democratic nominee for United States Senate (1978), but defeated by Republican incumbent Strom Thurmond; and Democratic nominee for Congress (1980), but defeated by Republican
Thomas Hartnett. Herbert Ravenel Sass was a short story writer,
often published in *The Saturday Evening Post* and other national
magazines.

Rebsomn
REB-sum

Most pre-Revolutionary settlers of this German family name translated their name to Turnipseed. Hans and Peat Rebsomn in 1752
owned land in upper Richland County on Cedar Creek where it
enters the Broad River. Other members of the family settled in
the area and served in Colonel Thomas Taylor's regiment in the
Revolution. (Colonel Taylor owned the plantation, Richland, that
in 1786 became the new capital city of Columbia.) In 1782 Jacob
Turnipseed owned land in the Camden area (Kershaw County,
northeast of present Columbia). In 1980 South Carolina had two
Turnipseed state senators, brothers Tom and David from Spar-

tanburg and Lexington, respectively. David is the much more sedate of the two. Tom was Democratic nominee for Congress in 1980, but was defeated by Republican incumbent Floyd Spence.

Rial
RIE-ul (rhymes with dial)

Rial Hill is a wooded elevation at the foot of the Blue Ridge Mountains on SC 8 between Easley and Pickens. The hill belonged to the Ariail family, late nineteenth-century settlers, and the name is a clipped version of the French family name.

Ribaut
ree-Boe, ree-BAW, ree-BOTE

Ribaut Road, one of the main streets of lowcountry Beaufort, is named for the early Huguenot leader Jean Ribaut. In 1562 he established his short-lived French colony Charlesfort on Parris Island in Port Royal Sound. Although ree-BAW is heard fairly often, when Kershaw Tom Peach went calling on his intended, May Dowling, in Beaufort, he got puzzled looks when he asked the location of ree-BAW Road; finally one of the older native folks clarified, "Some of the young ones just call it ree-BOAT, but most of us still prefer ree-BOE."

Rimini
RIM-i-NIE

On the border of Clarendon and Sumter counties, the town of Rimini is just east of an upper branch of Lake Marion. During the building of the railroad, an Italian logging crew gave this name to their work camp, from a seaport town in Italy. When the railroad and the loggers moved on, the name Rimini stayed, though pronounced differently from the Italian RIM-i-NEE (for example, Francesca of Rimini in Dante's *Divine Comedy*).

Roblyn
ROB-lin (rhymes with goblin)

Roblyn's Neck in Darlington County was a railroad stop in the ox-bow shaped bend of the Peedee River below Welsh Neck. It was named for Peter Roblyn, who received a land grant there in 1736. The land was later owned by Governor David Rogerson Williams (1776–1830), and more recently in 1968 by C. K. Dunlap of Hartsville. The railroad station has been abandoned, but the name survives in corrupted form as Robbin's Neck, with the ex post facto explanation that it's named for a bird haven.

Rough
ROW (rhymes with NOW)

The many ways this name has been mispronounced correspond to the various sounds that ough spells in the English language: cough, plough, tough, though, through, thought, and borough. The British family came from Cornwall in the nineteenth century to the Midwest, then to California, and after World War II to South Carolina. Albert James Rough is a district petroleum representative in Spartanburg, where Chris Rough is a professional artist.

Ruff
ROOF (OO as in boot)

The family names Ruff and Roof have the same pronunciation; but recently a newscaster pronounced Ruff to rhyme with cuff when announcing a meeting to be held at the State Fairgrounds' Ruff Building. The Newberry County town of Little Mountain was earlier called Ruff's Little Mountain after the owner of the nearby monadnock. For most of this century Ruff Hardware Company was a store on Columbia's Main Street. The Methodist Church in Ridgeway (US 21 and SC 34) was formerly called Ruff's Chapel for the family there. Mrs. William Herbert Ruff

(1860–1957) was grand lady of Long Leaf Plantation, built in the 1850s by her father, Colonel Henry Campbell Davis, and still in the Davis-Ruff family in Ridgeway.

Said
SED

No, it's not a French family's attempt to hide their sadistic forebear Marquis de Sade (1740–1814) via new spelling and different pronunciation. The Said Lands is an area in the Peedee region southwest of Florence (US 76 and US 52). For over 100 years it has been populated almost exclusively by blacks. During Reconstruction the land was divided into 40-acre plots and distributed to the newly freed slaves. The deeds referred to "the aforesaid lands," and the name Said Lands survives from this legal terminology.

Salley
SAL-li

The original spelling of this German family name, Sahly, might suggest a broad *a* (AH) pronunciation. Instead, it's pronounced like the woman's name. George Elmore Salley (1788–1828), planter, captain in the War of 1812, senator from Orangeburg District, gave 200 acres of land for and helped to build Poplar Springs Academy. A. S. Salley was for over 40 years state historian. The Aiken County town of Salley (SC 394 and SC 39) is known today for its annual Chit'lin Strut Festival.

Samaria
suh-MEH-ri-uh

According to Lexington County historian, Lee Gandee, "Samaria is hardly a village. Some say it is merely a state of mind. The people there, disgruntled by being passed over and ignored whenever public improvements were being made in other communities, took the Biblical name as a reproach to the rest of the county. Located near the old Tory Trail, now called Bootlegger Road, . . . Samaria still has the feeling that people consider it a place beyond the pale."

Sans Souci
SAHN SOO-si (OO as in boot)

Sans Souci was the Rutledge family plantation near Stateburg (SC 261 north of US 76) in Sumter County. The name is from the French, meaning without care or carefree—rather a misnomer since the Colonial-Revolutionary Rutledges were among the most responsible families in the state: Edward was a signer of the Declaration of Independence; John was president and then governor of South Carolina, chief justice of the state Court of Common Pleas, and Chief Justice of the United States; and Hugh and Edward together had a comfortable law practice for clients John was too busy to serve.

Saussey
SAW-si

This Columbia family of Swiss origin is spelled Saucy on some records. Colonel George S. Saussey, Jr., USMC (retired), now of Pawley's Island, is a teacher at Waccamaw Academy. George S. Saussey, III, is an environmental planner in Columbia. (See Seneca for Mrs. Flo Saussey.)

Saverance
SEV-runs (second syllable rhymes with once)

The Saverance family settled in Darlington in the Peedee, where the name still survives. Clifton R. Saverance and Warren G. Saverance, both graduates in agriculture from Clemson University, are now retired residents of Lamar. Donald W. Saverance is a state tax auditor in Columbia.

Sawney
SAW-ni

Sawney Creek, east of Ridgeway (US 21 and SC 34) in Fairfield County, flows south toward Columbia, then turns east toward the Wateree River. There are three suggested origins of this name: that Sawney is a form of the Indian Shawnee; that Sawney was the name of a family that settled in the area around 1800; and that in the eighteenth century Sawney was a word used to refer to a Scotsman, and one may have settled along the creek.

Saxe Gotha
SAKS-GAH-thuh

The area west of Columbia and southwest of the Saluda and Congaree rivers was named Saxe Gotha in the 1730s for the birth place of the daughter-in-law of King George II. It was so recorded on Cook's and Mouzon's maps. The area was largely settled by Germans. After the Revolution the name of Saxe Gotha was changed to Lexington, for the battle in Massachusetts—rather ironically since there were more battles in South Carolina than in Massachusetts or any other colony. Evidence of the early name survives in the Lexington County town of Red Bank, where Saxe Gotha is engraved on a stone marker on the grounds of what was once Red Bank Textile Mill. A magazine *Saxe Gotha* was a short-lived publication of Bruner Publishers in 1973. In reverence for their German heritage, the Lutheran Synod adopted the name Saxe Gotha for their church organization in 1978.

Schumacher
SHOO-MAKE-uh (OO as in boot)

This name of German origin has been respelled Shoemaker by some of the family. Schumacher is one of many German names in the northwest town of Walhalla (SC 183 and SC 28), settled in 1850 by the German Colonization Society of Charleston. Snead

Schumacher is a civil engineer in Walhalla. Alan Hoyt Shoemaker is a zoologist in Columbia.

Scoville
SKOE-vul

Scoville Street in Orangeburg is named for the prominent family there. Joseph A. Scoville was private secretary to John C. Calhoun at the time of his death (1854). Phillips L. Scoville, Greer businessman, lives in Greenville. Jack Miller Scoville, Jr., has been an officer in the R. L. Bryan Company of Columbia.

Screven
SKRIV-en

The family name, still prevalent throughout the state, has sometimes been spelled Scriven. Landgrave Thomas Smith willed to his daughter Mary Scriven part of his Wiskinboo land, secured in 1689 between the Cooper and Santee rivers. In 1698 the Reverend William Screven, from England, was the first Baptist missionary in the Carolinas. He secured 804 acres of land west of Biggin Creek (off SC 6 near the village of Pinopolis; Biggin Creek is one of the headwaters of Cooper estuary). According to the 1860 Federal Census of Beaufort District, John Henry Screven of Castle Hill Plantation in Prince William's Parish and Dr. Thomas Edward Screven of St. Peter's Parish each owned more than 100 slaves. The mother of DuBose Heyward, author of *Porgy*, was a Screven.

Seay
SEE

James H. Seay, a minister, in 1850 built his large two-story colonial home in lower Richland County four miles north of Eastover near the old Garner's Ferry Road (US 76) to Sumter. The Bynum-Seay cemetery in the area is east of the Nutshell Plantation house. The Seay name is prevalent in the Midlands. James Thomas Seay is a Columbia building contractor. His son Jim Seay is sportscaster for WSCQ radio and suggests that his name may be a different spelling and pronunciation of the Irish Sean.

Sedalia
suh-DAE-li-uh

The upcountry town of Sedalia is between Enoree and Tyger rivers east of Cross Keys (SC 49). In Union County, Sedalia was probably named by the Quakers for a place in Ireland. It was once a crossroads on a stagecoach route where the Quakers had their Friends Meeting House.

Seneca
SEN-e-KUH

The Indian word may mean miracle or blue snake root. Seneca was the most southerly of Cherokee villages and is now the town (SC 130 and SC 28, off US 123) south of Lake Keowee in the northwestern county of Oconee. Pronunciations can often separate residents from "visitors," as evidenced by a Seneca story: Mrs. Flo Saussey unexpectedly returned from Columbia to her home in Highlands, North Carolina, across the state line from Oconee County. A young girl had broken into the Saussey house and for some time had been making herself at home. To Mrs. Saussey's question, "Where do you come from?" the intruder responded, "su-NEEK-uh." And Mrs. Saussey quickly concluded, "Oh, no, you don't—not if you pronounce it that way."

Shannon
SHAN-nun

Shannon Hill (US 15) is about half a mile from Lynches River bridge near Bishopville in Lee County. It was the site of the last fatal duel fought in South Carolina, the Shannon-Cash duel (July 5, 1880), in which Colonel William M. Shannon was killed by Colonel E. B. C. Cash. Since before the turn of the century Shannon Town has been the name of the black residential section just southeast of Sumter, but no Shannons live there nor have they been landowners there during this century.

Shealy
SHEE-li

The original German was Schele. The family, in the Dutch Fork since 1730, now spells its name Shealy, Shealey, or Sheely, but not Shelley—that's an English-origin family. Today, however the name is spelled, there are more Schele descendants than Smiths in the Greater Columbia telephone directory. In the late 1960s Sherry Shealy from Lexington County was the youngest woman ever elected to the state legislature. C. Eston Shealy, mayor of Chapin (US 76, off I 26), has been a town official for over fifteen years. Willie Curtis Sheely, Jr., was an educator and accountant in Ballentine (US 76, off I 26). Melba Shealy is an active family genealogist.

Sherard
SHEH-rud

Though some may deem it more modern to say shuh-RAHRD, the family that's been in the state over 175 years still prefers SHEH-rud. Alexander Sherard came from Northern Ireland to present Anderson County in 1801. He had four sons and his son John had seven sons, so that the name is still prominent in the upcountry Anderson-Abbeville-Greenwood area. William Sherard, another son of immigrant Alexander, was one of the five commissioners named in 1828 to select the site of the courthouse for the newly established Anderson County (named for Revolutionary Colonel Robert Anderson).

Shivar

SHIE-vuh

Though the water from Shivar Springs was mighty cool, neither the spelling nor the pronunciation is related to the shiver from the cold. Shivar Springs, near Shelton on the Broad River in Fairfield County, was on the Southern Railway about halfway between Columbia and Spartanburg. The springs were owned and developed as a business around 1908 by N. P. Shivar. They were commended by the state House of Representatives "for the excellent quality of water furnished during the session of 1909" and were recommended "to all who are in need of a pure mineral water of medicinal properties." Shivar water and Shivar ginger ale were for over 25 years bottled and sold throughout the United States. Springs and "spaws" of the state had long been widely publicized, as noted in Thomas Lockwood's *A Geography of South Carolina* (1832).

Siau

SEE-oe

The Harold Siau Bridge (first called Lafayette Bridge) connecting Waccamaw Neck and Pawley's Island was completed in 1935. The bridge was named for L. H. Siau, who in 1935 was Public Works Administrator of Georgetown County. The Siau family has long been in the mid-coastal area. In 1825 Lewis Siau and Company advertised a booth at the Georgetown races where there would be available dinners and the best assortment of liquors. The races were sponsored by the Georgetown Jockey Club.

Simons

SIM-unz, SIE-munz

Simons spelled with a single "m" is French Huguenot, but even some of them have given in to the long I pronunciation of the name. Either pronunciation is a long way from the French; as one of the Huguenot Carolinians noted, "I've been called SIM-unz for so long that I might not even answer if someone called me SEE-MOE." The Jewish name Simons is always pronounced with the long I, SIE-munz. A favorite among the French Huguenot descendants, Katherine Drayton Mayrant Simons (1890–1969), as Drayton Mayrant, wrote two volumes of poetry and nine historical novels, and was a contributing editor of *Names in South Carolina*. The Simmon Tree was a popular gathering place in the upcountry Pea Ridge section of Union County. But neither the Simons nor Simmons families can claim credit for the name of the spot where people would congregate for over 50 years "to trade, traffic, gossip, and drink." The name resulted from Southerners' tendency to abbreviate the persimmon tree to 'Simmon Tree. The tree's gone now, but the old-timers still remember.

Skyagunsta
SKIE-uh-GUN-stuh

The Indian word means wizard owl or wise owl. Skyagunsta was the laudatory name given by the Cherokee Indians to their friend General Andrew Pickens, one of the state's three most prominent Revolutionary generals (the other two were Francis Marion and Thomas Sumter). As a devout official in the Presbyterian Church, Pickens was also nicknamed the Fighting Elder.

Smoak
SMOKE

Our English-origin names have stayed pretty much the same in spelling, though pronunciations may vary a bit; our French-origin names have been pronounced differently from the French or perhaps phonetically spelled; but our German-origin names have often been respelled beyond recognition or even translated to the English equivalent. So it is with Smoak. Originally Rauch, most of the families over the state have long used the translation Smoak, though the spelling is less fiery than the pronunciation. The town of Smoaks (US 21 and SC 217) in lowcountry Colleton County is named for the early German settlers.

Smyth(e)
SMITHE (long I)

With or without the final e, the name, contrasting with Smith, is pronounced with the long I, SMITHE. Gresham Smyth of Yemassee (SC 68), south of the Combahee River, served in the state House and Senate from Prince William Parish (1814–1822). Augustine Thomas Smythe, Senator from Charleston County (1880–1894), was the father-in-law of poet-novelist John Bennett.

Snowden
SNOW-dun, SNOE-dun

Princess Margaret's ex-husband Lord Snowden properly gave his title the icy pronunciation. And just as properly the history professor, newspaper writer and poet, Yates Snowden, preferred his name to have the NOW-rhyming first syllable. Snowden possessed a fine library and to keep it intact he held an annual party, requiring that each guest bring back a book he'd borrowed and not borrow another one that evening. One of the honeycomb buildings on University of South Carolina's Columbia campus, Snowden dormitory recognizes this colorful man. Regrettably, most students who live in the building named for Yates ignore his preference in pronunciation. Snowdens is a black community near Mount Pleasant on the coast midway between the Wando River and US 17. It is named for the Snowden family that owned a large plantation there up to 1861. More recently come to South Carolina are Snowden families that pronounce the name icily, like Lord Snowden. They too are right. And the rightest of these is Marian Elizabeth Snowden of West Columbia who in 1980 graduated summa cum laude in civil engineering.

Socastee
SOK-us-tee

It may be an Indian word meaning house or wash. The town of
Socastee in Horry County is eleven miles west of Myrtle Beach
at the intersection of SC 544 and SC 707. Socastee Swamp, flowing
into Waccamaw River about twelve miles south of Conway, was
the scene of a Revolutionary battle in January 1781.

Sompayrac
SUMP-RAK

The Sompayrac family came to Darlington in the Peedee area
around 1830. In 1976 Hewitt A. Sompayrac published an excellent
little pamphlet entitled *Society Hill, Welsh Neck, Long Bluff, Old
Greenville,* intended as a preview to his forthcoming book-length
history of the area. In his introduction he praises the character of
the Sompayracs, Cokers, and other early settlers there: ". . . a
sturdy group who made the wild tame, the soft strong, the aver-
age great, the insecure secure, the unknown known, and gave
South Carolina a backbone."

Sorghum
SOHR-gum

Sorghum is a dark syrup made from the sorgo reed plant and
resembles the sweeter, less thick cane syrup. Camp Sorghum
(nicknamed for its molasses diet) was established in 1864 by the
Confederates as a prison camp for federal officers. The camp was
located in West Columbia in what is now the Saluda Gardens
residential suburb. Ben Dekle, WCAY Cayce radio personality
of the 1970s, frequently reminded his listeners that he lived on
Sorghum Hill.

Spigner
SPIGE-nuh (long I, hard G)

For all its spellings—Spigner, Spigener, Spegner, Spaegner—the name, of German origin, is usually pronounced SPIGE-nuh. The Spigners of the Midlands were pre-Revolutionary landowners in lower Richland County, east of present Columbia. Frederick Spigner served under Colonel Thomas Taylor in the Revolution. In the twentieth century, Adolphus Fletcher Spigner, father and son, were both Columbia attorneys and state senators from Richland County. Their cousin, Hubert Spigner, was a very popular teacher at University High School and professor in the English Department of the University of South Carolina.

Sproull
SPRUL

The James Sproull family came from Ireland to Newberry County around 1790. Son James bought a plantation along Five Notch Road in the southern part of what is now Greenwood County. The plantation had been previously owned by the Harrison family of Troy (SC 10, off US 221).

Steadman
STED-mun

The town in Lexington County was titled Steedman or sometimes Stedman in the 1880s and Steadman after 1899. For all three spellings, the family name is pronounced with the short e, whether it's our informant Joseph E. Steadman, Sr., of Lexington County or Marguerite Couturier Steedman of Charleston. George Steedman, son of a Scotch-Irish immigrant, came to Lexington in 1785. His house was called "Steadman's Folly." The house and Steadman's large acreage were on a tributary stream of the north fork of Edisto River (SC 178) about ten miles below Batesburg. The town of Steedman, two miles west of the family home, grew up

around the mill and store established in 1860 by grandson John
Marcellus Steedman.

Stoll
STAWL

Stoll's Alley runs east-west for one block between Church and
Bay streets in Charleston. The pronunciation apparently confuses
even Charlestonians since the street sign reads Stoll, but the
bronze marker on the sidewalk reads Stalls. The alley is named
for Justinius Stoll, who owned land there in 1762.

Stoudemire
STOW-duh-MIRE; STOO-duh-MIRE
(first syllable rhymes with NOW) (OO as in boot)

The name and both pronunciations are prevalent in the state,
especially in the Midlands. Many of the family descend from the
early German settlers in Orangeburg. The pronunciation is apparently a matter of personal choice—even members of the same
family may differ. And then there's the family that spells the name
with an extra letter, Stoudenmire. They prefer the oo-as-in-boot
pronunciation. Mrs. H. O. Stoudenmire lives at upcountry Lake
Lanier, Landrum. Mrs. Betty Jean Stoudemire was recently
elected to South Congaree town council.

Strother
STRAH-thuh

William Strother was state senator from Fairfield District (1810–
1812) and served as a major in the War of 1812. Strother was a
station on the Southern Railway in Fairfield County, on SC 34 just
below the bridge across the Broad River. Richard Strother of
Newberry and Dr. Solomon P. Strother owned the land there.
Strothers were also early settlers in Orangeburg District. Now

Strother is occasionally used as a given name, as with Dr. Strother Pope, Columbia physician, and the late sheriff of Richland County, Strother Sligh.

Sugaw
SHOO-guh (OO as in put)

It's an Indian word possibly meaning house. Sugaw Creek, part of the boundary between North and South Carolina, runs southeast toward the Catawba River. Homemade booze apparently accounted for the inverted V in the bounary line there: the surveyors were following the creek as instructed when they heard of a good liquor still some ten miles north of the other side of the stream. Measuring chains and all, they visited the still for a happy hour. Then they headed back south a few miles downstream to the prescribed boundary markings. That detour is the reason that the triangle including Fort Mill north of Sugaw Creek is in South Carolina instead of North Carolina. Several years later attempts were made to have the boundary line follow the creek bed as intended. But one of the most landed citizens in Fort Mill is said to have objected with good reason, "No, siree. It's too cold in North Carolina. I'd rather live in the warmer state just like I been doing." Pre-Revolutionary Sugaw Creek Academy was forerunner of the first institution of higher learning south of Virginia, Queen's Museum, later called Liberty Hall, in Charlotte, North Carolina.

Swansea
SWAHN-si

Though we have occasionally heard SWAHN-SEE and SWAHN-SEE-uh, the vast majority, at home and abroad, prefer SWAHN-si. The Lexington County town of Swansea (US 321 and SC 6) is twenty miles south of Columbia. The origin of the name is hard to pin down. In the Bicentennial celebration (1976) the town's publicity releases claimed Swansea in Wales as its parent city. But since there are no records of Welsh settlers in that part of

Lexington, it's a bit far-fetched to assert such a connection. And then there's the suggestion that Swansea is a family name. Records of the eighteenth and nineteenth centuries reveal family names in Lexington County like Swansy, Swanzy, Swanzey; but these families were way over in the Dutch Fork section. Perhaps the most interesting but also undocumented story is of the German storekeeper who operated on the trail from Charleston. Travelers stopping at the store would ask how many miles to Friday's Ferry (on the Congaree River across from present Columbia). And the German storekeeper would respond in broken English: "How many mile? Zwansig"—the German word for twenty. By folk etymology, Zwansig became Swansea, the present name of the town. And there's the story of the settler who built a pond for his two swans—a swan sea; or some say Swansea may be a respelling of an Indian word.

Sylvan
SIL-VAN

Newcomers too often think the natives don't know that the adjective meaning wooded or filled with trees is pronounced SIL-vun, and so they call one of the longest tree-laden roads in Columbia's North Trenholm suburb SIL-vun Drive. But what they don't know is that, with or without trees, Sylvan Drive is named for the longtime Columbia jeweler's family, whose name we and the Sylvans pronounce SIL-VAN.

Talbert, Tolbert
TAHL-but

It's pronounced the same, whether it's Putter Talbert, Carolina coed of the 1940s, or Tieless Joe Tolbert of South Carolina's Republican Party several decades earlier—when there hardly was one.

Taliaferro
TAHL-uh-vuh

It's a Virginia and South Carolina name, pronounced the same as Tolliver. Dick Taliaferro, later a prominent physician, was a star football player at Columbia High School and Duke University in the 1930s.

Tamassee
tuh-MAH-si

Tamassee is a town in the northwestern corner of the state on SC 11. The name was also given to General Andrew Pickens' home and to the Daughters of the American Revolution Industrial School built at the site. It's an Indian word meaning sunlight of god and referring to a red gem possessed by an Indian medicine man, to whom the gem was believed to give great power. At his death, as he had instructed, he was buried with the gem in his hand. Ever after the place of his burial has been called Tamassee, as was the Revolutionary battle fought there in August 1781.

Tarcote
TEHR-kote

It looks French, but it isn't. Tarcote Swamp (also spelled Tar' Coat) is a tributary of the Black River in lowcountry Clarendon County just below where US 301 crosses the river near Manning. The name dates from the Revolution when Francis Marion's men were chasing Redcoats through the swamp. The story handed down is that one of the British escapees tore his coat, leaving a part on some briars and thorns—thus the original name Tear Coat Swamp, through the years variously pronounced and spelled Tare Coat, Tarcote, Tarcoat, and now often Tar' Coat (with the *ar* as in *air*).

Tega Cay
TEE-guh KAE

This cay (key—here a small islet) is on Lake Wylie near the North Carolina line going toward Carowinds and Charlotte, North Carolina. In 1982 the recently developed residential community received status as a municipality, the 265th in the state.

Theus
THEE-us (like the TH in theatre)

The Rev. Christian Theus, Presbyterian minister, preached in the Midlands' Saxe Gotha (now Lexington County) for fifty years (1739–1789). His brother Jeremiah Theus of Charleston achieved considerable fame as one of the best Colonial painters. Two members of the Theus family were officers in the South Carolina Continentals during the Revolution.

Tobias
TOE-BIE-us

The name is still present in the state, especially from Columbia to Charleston. Joseph Tobias (1685–1761) served the South Carolina Colonial government as a Spanish interpreter during the conflict with Spain in Florida (1739–1745). He was also a prominent merchant-shipper and one of the founders and first president of Charleston's Beth Elohim Synagogue, established 1749. Thomas Jefferson Tobias, a descendant of Joseph, is author of several historical works, including *The Hebrew Orphan Society of Charleston* and *The Hebrew Benevolent Society of Charleston*. Pat Tobias and Company is a real estate firm in Columbia.

Towe
TOW (rhymes with NOW)

The Towe family settled in lower Richland County, and the name still survives in the Midlands. Arthur Towe, Jr., lives in West Columbia, and M. C. Towe is in nearby Cayce.

Trenholm
TREN-um

Trenholm Road in eastern Columbia is named for the family whose antebellum home was there. George A. Trenholm of Columbia was treasurer of the Confederacy.

Trezevant
TREZ-VANT

Daniel Trezevant, French Huguenot, came to South Carolina soon after the Revocation of the Edict of Nantes in 1685 and settled around 1694 at Orange Quarter near the Cooper River. The name survives both as a family name and as a given name. Arthur Trezevant Wayne of Oakland Plantation near Mount Pleasant was a distinguished ornithologist.

Trio
TRIE-OE

This post office in southeastern Williamsburg County is pronounced TRI-OE, even though it was named for a trio of men: W. D. Bryan, W. R. Bryan, and James Bryan. The little town is south of the Black River and US 521 between Lane and Andrews.

Tugaloo
TUG-uh-LOO (OO as in boot)

It's an Indian word meaning two, but two what? Or it may mean
fork in a stream or white-fronted goose. Prather's Covered Bridge,
pre-dating the Civil War, joined Westminster, South Carolina,
and Toccoa, Georgia, over the Tugaloo River on county road 17,
five miles north of US 123 in northwestern Oconee County. The
Tugaloo River is one of the headwaters of the Savannah River.

Tunander
too-NAN-duh (oo as in rule)

William Adrian Tunander, born in Falun, Sweden, came to Columbia around 1897. His forebear Thunander had gone to Sweden
from the south of France. The Tunander home, on the National
Register of Historic Places, is at 1426 Hampton Street in Columbia. It is the residence of Miss Martha E. Tunander.

Tuomey
TOO-mi (OO as in rule; rhymes with gloomy)

Of Irish origin, Tuomey family members have long been promi-
nent benefactors in Sumter (east of Columbia). Sumter's Tuomey
Hospital is named for the family. St. Anne's Catholic Church, of
Gothic design, on Sumter's East Liberty Street, was completed in
1909 through legacies of Mrs. Alice W. Poole and Mrs. Ella
Tuomey.

Turbeville, Turbyfill
TUHR-buh-vul

The area (US 378 and 301) between Sumter and Lake City was
originally called Puddin' Swamp, perhaps for the mushy land
thereby. The railroad station and express office were named Seloc

(not Indian, just the backward spelling of Coles, a family who lived there) until service was discontinued in 1895. Michael Turbeville settled in the area in 1840. The town grew up in the 1870s around the general store and turpentine mill operated by Michael's sons, William and Clem. As a postal address, the community officially became Turbeville in 1898. The name is now widespread over the state. Those who spelled it Turbyfill included an excellent first grade teacher at Satchel Ford School in Columbia.

Tuscarora
TUS-kuh-ROH-ruh

Tuscarora Jack Barnwell earned his nickname when he served as Captain of the South Carolina force sent to help defeat the rampaging Tuscarora Indians in North Carolina in 1711. He was the immigrant founder of the prominent Barnwell family for whom the town (US 278 and SC 70) and the county bordering the Savannah River are named.

Urquhart
UHR-kut

Urquhart Station is the South Carolina Electric and Gas Company power plant on the Savannah River. It was named for Norman D. Urquhart, supervisor of its construction and chief construction engineer for the power company. From another branch of the family, James Burwell Urquhart (1876–1961) came to Columbia from South Hampton, Virginia, in 1900 as a civil engineer with the Seaboard Railway. He served as architect for the city schools and the housing authority. His two daughters are Alice (Mrs. Rufus R. Clark) and Aimee (Mrs. Jessie T. Rees). The Urquhart name is of Scottish origin.

168

Utsey

YOOT-si (OO as in booze; rhymes with cutsie)

The Utsey family, of German origin, settled in lower South Carolina in the St. George area (US 15 and US 78) of Dorchester County. Mrs. Donald Russell, Sr., was Virginia Utsey, native of St. George. Dr. Robert Daniel Utsey, Sr., also a St. George native, practices dentistry in West Columbia.

Vanderhorst

VAN DRAWS; VAN-duh HOHRST
(DRAWS rhymes with sauce)

Of Dutch origin, Arnoldus Vander Horst (1748–1815), Charleston planter, was a captain in the Revolution under General Francis Marion. He served in various political capacities, including terms as senator and governor. His Vanderhorst Wharf could store 5,000 bags of cotton. The street in Charleston is pronounced VAN DRAWS. The street in Winnsboro is pronounced VAN-duh-HOHRST. Charlestonian John Vanderhorst owned much of the land in Fairfield that was to become Winnsboro. The same John was one of the buyers of lots of the newly established capital city of Columbia. Vanderhorst Mansion, built about 1719 on Kiawah Island, is on one of the South Carolina tours. The island was owned by the Vanderhorst family for 180 years. In 1952 the island was sold to C. C. Royal Lumber Company of Aiken for $125,000; in 1974 the same island was sold to Kuwait Investment Corporation for $17,300,000. A black minister of the name in Georgetown answers to the phonetic pronunciation VAN-duh-HOHRST.

Van Wyck

van-WIKE

The town of Van Wyck (SC 75), southeast of Rock Hill, is in Lancaster County in the triangle that juts into North Carolina, just across Sugaw Creek. It's the only town in the United States called Van Wyck. The community was first called Heath. In 1887 the Seaboard Railway established a station there. General Hoke, a company official, named the station Van Wyck, his wife's maiden name. Near Van Wyck, Ashe's Ferry on Catawba River was the last public ferry in the state, discontinuing service about 1970.

Varennes
vuh-REN-nis

The French name for this upcountry town in Anderson County means wasteland. Legend has it that a French storekeeper at the crossroads where Varennes is located gave the name from his homeland: in those hills of France he'd left his sweetheart when he came to America. Varennes Presbyterian Church was organized in 1813 by the Rev. Richard B. Cater, but it has moved its location several times and is now at Iva (SC 184 and SC 81). There is also a Varennes Tavern in the area.

Vaucluse
VAW-KLOOZ (OO as in boot)

The little town of Vaucluse (SC 191 south of I 20) in Aiken County is northwest of Aiken. The name is from Vaucluse Plantation there, the word being Spanish, meaning beautiful. The plantation, property of Laura Allen, was part of her marriage settlement to Dr. John Saffold Stoney in 1861.

Verdery
VUHR-dri

The upcountry town of Verdery (SC 10) is in the Promised Land section southwest of Greenwood. It was named for a prominent Augusta, Georgia, businessman who was an official for the railroad being built through the area, most recently called the Charleston and Western Carolina Railroad. T. Mark Verdery in his undergraduate days wrote on "Indian-Named Rivers" for *Names in South Carolina* (1969); he is now a Presbyterian clergyman in Alabama.

Verdier

veh-DEEHR

The John Mark Verdier house (built about 1790) at 801 Bay Street, Beaufort, was visited by the Marquis de Lafayette in 1795. It is now a museum operated by the Historic Beaufort Foundation. The James Robert Verdier house, also in Beaufort at 501 Pinckney Street, is one of the locales of Francis Griswold's novel, *A Sea Island Lady.*

Videau

vee-DOE

General Francis Marion married his first cousin, Mary Ester Videau of St. John's Berkeley, in 1786. There were no children and therefore no direct descendants of these two French Huguenots. Videau Legare Beckwith Kirk (Mrs. Francis Marion Kirk) of Columbia is a collateral descendant.

Vienna

VIE-EN-uh

Though you may properly speak of vee-EN-uh, Austria, when you're in these parts you'd better check with the natives. Upcountry Abbevillians call their street VIE-EN-uh. In early days it was the road leading to similarly pronounced Vienna on the Savannah River. That town was destined to become a river port city for shipping cotton downstream to Savannah and Charleston. But the railroads came and Vienna, South Carolina, died before its time. The present Georgia town of Vienna (also pronounced VIE-EN-uh) is 'way over in South Georgia.

Villepigue
VIL-i-PIG

Of French descent, Confederate General John B. Villepigue was from Camden in Kershaw County—the only county in the state to furnish six generals to the Confederacy. The other five were James Cantey, James Chesnut, Zach Canty Deas, J. D. Kennedy, and Joseph Brevard Kershaw. Villepigue Extension, a street in Camden, is named for three family members each of whom served in a different war: the general of the Confederate War; Cantey, recipient of the Congressional Medal of Honor for service in World War I; and John of the U.S. Navy, who died in World War II.

Villepontoux
VIL-uh-PUN-TOE

It's a French Huguenot family name still present in Charleston and also spelled Villeponteux. Villepontoux Branch in lowcountry Berkeley County was named for Zachariah Villepontoux, vestryman of St. James Goose Creek. His plantation Mt. Parnassus was on Back River, where he made bricks used for Charleston's St. Michael's Church. Pontoux Branch is also named for the Villepontoux family. Peter Villepontoux was granted a patent in 1733 for a machine he had invented for cleaning rice.

Vingt et un
TWEN-ti WUN

It is easier for Southerners to use the English translation than to attempt the French pronunciation. Vingt et un was a Rees family plantation near Wedgefield (SC 261 and SC 763), west of Sumter. Tradition has it that the name-giver won the lands in a card game of Twenty-One, and commemorated his good luck with the French name.

Visanska
vi-ZAN-ski

G. A. Visanska came to upcountry Abbeville in 1872. His family so prospered as merchants and planters, in partnership with the Rosenbergs, that the two families were called the Rothschilds of Abbeville. Dr. Sam Visanska became one of the first pediatricians in the Southeast. Morton Visanska and other family members were prominent in musical and theatrical circles in Columbia.

Vogel
VOE-gul

Vogel is a German-origin family name still present in the Dutch Fork (Newberry County) and Orangeburg areas, where some have taken the name Fogle. The Germanic name Vogelgesang has been literally translated by some families to Birdsong. Appropriately the weathervane cock and bells atop St. John's Lutheran Church in Charleston were donated in the 1960s by Dr. Richard Haymaker as a memorial to his mother, whose maiden name was Vogelgesang. The happen-so story of this memorial is told in an article, "A Footnote That Changed the Charleston Skyline," *Georgia Review*, Fall 1965.

von Lehe
vahn LEE

The German-origin family name of von Lehe is well known in lower Richland County and Walterboro in Colleton County.

Waddel, Waddell
wah-DEL

Dr. Moses Waddel reputedly pronounced his name WAHD-uhl; this is supported by the story that he once remarked, "Well, I've waddled all my life, and I'll waddle to the end." However, now the name—even his—is usually pronounced wah-DEL. The Moses Waddel Academy (1804–1819) was in old Abbeville District near the town of Willington, now in McCormick County (SC 81). Operated by the renowned teacher and Presbyterian minister, Willington Academy (its official title) turned out several students who later served their state and nation. Three of these were John C. Calhoun, who entered the junior class at Yale; and George McDuffie, who graduated first honor from South Carolina College; and A. B. Longstreet, president of the University of South Carolina and author of *Georgia Scenes* and *Master William Mitten*, the latter being a novel based on his experience at Waddel's Academy. The present state senator James Madison Waddell of Beaufort was born in Arkansas.

Wagener

WAG-nuh

The German family name Wagener is pronounced the same as the name spelled Wagner. The town of Wagener (SC 302) is about halfway between Columbia and Aiken. It is named either for F. W. Wagener, traveling merchant of the late 1800s, or for George W. Wagener, Charleston merchant who promoted the building of the railroad between Wagener and Perry. The town had been previously called Pender Town and Gunter's Crossroads. The annual Wagons to Wagener Festival has been held every first weekend in May since 1970, featuring industrial exhibits, one- and five-mile running events, and arts and crafts. General John A. Wagener, mayor of Charleston, promoted and helped finance the German Colonization Society (1848), from which a group of settlers traveled upcountry to establish the Oconee County town of Walhalla. A monument to General Wagener was erected in the town. In 1840 Wagener was elected first president of the newly formed St. Matthews Lutheran Church in Charleston. A grandson of the Walhalla founder, William Yeaton ("Dutch") Wagener was tennis coach and popular professor of American literature at the University of South Carolina.

Walhalla
wahl-HAH-luh

The town of Walhalla (SC 183 and SC 28) in Oconee County in the northwest corner of the state was settled by the German Colonization Society, promoted by John Andreas Wagener. The name is from Norse mythology, Walhalla, or Valhalla, being the hall of the gods. Walhalla's College Street commemorates three colleges in the town during the nineteenth century: Newberry College, 1868–1877; Walhalla Female College, 1877–1885; Adger College, about 1873–1883.

Waller
WAH-luh

Swearing Jack Waller (1741–1802) was a locally famous Baptist preacher and founder of several churches in present upcountry Laurens and Greenwood counties. Across the state and well over a century later Senator John Henry Waller, Jr., from Marion County was elected a circuit-court judge in 1980. Methodist Judge Waller is a less vocal Christian than was Swearing Jack of Baptist persuasion.

Wappoo
WAH-poo (oo as in boot)

Wappoo is an Indian word that may mean water. Wappoo Creek and Elliott Cut connect the Ashley and Stono rivers near the coast west of Charleston. It was near Wappoo Creek that Eliza Lucas, who was later to marry Chief Justice Charles Pinckney and to be the mother of Charles Cotesworth, Harriott, and Thomas Pinckney, experimented with the culture of indigo on her father's plantations. Her success led to the establishment of indigo as a staple crop for the colony until the Revolution. The tale is told in *Eliza of Wappoo* by Nell Saunders Graydon.

Wasbee
WUZ-bee

The unknowing have called Wasbee Range in Charleston WAS-BEE. Researchers could well spend much time trying to find evidence of the lost tribe of Wasbee Indians. But there was none. Wasbee Range was originally called Bee Range, for Confederate General Bernard Bee. (A range is a small, short street or alley.) There is also a more prominent thoroughfare (especially wide for Charleston) titled Bee Street. Records show that city council decided that duplicate names should be avoided for roads, streets, lanes, alleys, and ranges. As a result, what was Bee Range became Wasbee Range. Other duplications were similarly corrected: Motte Lane became Motley Lane; Michel Lane became Shell Lane; and Lee Street became Notlee Street.

Wassamassaw
WAH-suh-MAH-suh

This Indian word, spelled the same way backwards as forwards, may mean cane-ground river or place of connecting water. Wassamassaw Swamp in lowcountry Berkeley County is at the head of Cypress Swamp, which empties into the Ashley River. Mr. and Mrs. Jay Potter and family live five miles from the swamp and nearby Wassamassaw Baptist Church.

Waties
WAE-tis

Waties Island is from the French Huguenot name. Some maps, pronunciations, and legends to the contrary, it is not Waiters Island "because it is shaped like a serving tray." It is South Carolina's most northeastern coastal island, at the mouth of Little River on the North Carolina line. It is named for William Waties, the Indian trader to whom it was deeded in 1726 by Landgrave Thomas Smith. William Waties' great-granddaughter Catherine

Waties (1795–1855) married Colonel Orlando Savage Rees (1796–1852) of Stateburg—for whom Orlando, Florida, is named. Elizabeth Waties Allston Pringle (alias Patience Pennington) is author of *A Woman Rice Planter* and *Chronicles of Chicora Wood*—both accounts of her life on lowcountry plantations. J. Waties Waring, Charleston circuit court judge, was responsible for some early, precedent-setting decisions on blacks' right to vote in primary elections. The Waties name survives. John Waties Thomas, Columbia attorney, and Mary Waties (Way-Way) Lumpkin Pope (wife of Newberry attorney Thomas Pope) are grandchildren of Mary Waties Thomas (Mrs. John Peyre Thomas).

Wauchope
WAW-kup

It's a Scottish family name. George Armstrong Wauchope, long-time professor of English, wrote the words for the University of South Carolina alma mater, *We Hail Thee, Carolina*. His son Robert is an archeologist at Tulane University. His daughter Virginia is married to Robert Duncan Bass, biographer of Francis Marion and Thomas Sumter.

Whisenhunt
WHIZ-nunt

The original German spelling of this name was Ysenhut. J. W. Whisenhunt and Sons, Inc., is a large pork-producing operation in the Bolentown community in Orangeburg County and is managed by Whisenhunt brothers Clyde, Johnny, and Donnie. The late Henry S. Whisenhunt, Sr., was a farmer who lived nearby, a mile outside of the town of Cope.

Whooping
HOO-pin (OO as in booze)

Whooping Island has nothing to do with the endangered species
of crane. Located in the Edisto Island area south of Charleston,
Whooping Island was very important to the Edisto island folk
prior to the bridge's being built across the Dawhoo River in 1918.
Here the people who'd been visiting on the mainland would
whoop for the ferryman to come take them back home to Edisto.

Wienges
WIN-jiz

Othniel Wienges, former state legislator, is co-owner of Singleton
Plantation in Calhoun County out from St. Matthews (US 601
and SC 6). His sister Anne Wienges taught high school English
in upcountry York in the early 1940s. Wienges Lake is on Buck-
head Creek in Calhoun County.

Wier
WEH-uh

Thomas Wier (1763–1851) came from Scotland to Little River
in Laurens County, and then moved on to Greenwood (US 178
and SC 72), where he was a member of Rock Presbyterian Church.
His descendant, William Wier wrote *Ten Tribes of Wier*, a family
history tracing "the Wiers from Whence, the Wiers to Whither."
He recounts that just after the Civil War his grandmother stepped
onto her kitchen porch to empty her dishpan and found a young
black man in a cast-off Yankee uniform who asked, "Whah's
Wire?"

"Who?" asked Grandma.

"Wire—I got a paper to serve————"

Grandma Wier's answer to this mispronouncer was to douse him
with greasy dishwater, and after that she "lit on him with the
pan."

Wingard

WING-ud; WIN-GAHRD

It's a family name of German origin prominent in the Midlands of South Carolina. When Little League ballplayer Eddie Wingard answered to WIN-GAHRD, an old-timer asked him wasn't it WING-ud, and Eddie said it really didn't matter. But it used to. Anyone worth his salt from the Dutch Fork insisted on WING-ud; today you have to check with the owner. Current Wingards include Phillip Kirton Wingard, a lawyer in Lexington. William F. Wingard is a Lutheran minister. Melissa Connelly Wingard is a 1980 graduate in nursing from the Medical University of South Carolina. Virginia Wingard Memorial United Methodist Church is on Broad River Road near Dutch Square Shopping Center, northwest of Columbia.

Wisacky

WIE-SAK-i

The town of Wisacky in Lee County is on SC 341, six miles from Bishopville. It was first called Crane's Crossroads for Dr. Charles Crane, who owned property there. Then it was Cooterborough: the tiplers at the crossroads store often got so drunk that they had to crawl home on all fours like a cooter (cooter is the local name for turtle). Before the white settlers came, the Indian campground nearby had been called Wisackee; the word may mean cane. When the railroad was built through the area, R. M. Cooper, Sr., was asked to name the post office. He submitted the old Indian name Wisackee. Officious Washington "improved" the spelling so that since that date (1888) it's been Wisacky.

wisteria

wis-TEH-ri-uh; wis-TEEH-ri-uh

The early spring-blooming vines of lavender or white sweet-smelling grapelike clusters of flowers are profuse throughout woods and yards over the state. Both pronunciations are used, though wis-TEH-ri-uh may be the more citified.

Witherspoon
WITH-*uh*-SPOON (OO as in boot)

The Witherspoon family that settled before the Revolution near Kingstree in Williamsburg County were Scottish Protestants who had suffered religious persecution in Scotland and came to South Carolina after having settled briefly in Ireland. Their neighbors were mostly Irish Protestants, and the county was named for the Protestant king William III. The name of Witherspoon now is found throughout the state. Witherspoon's Ferry across Lynch's Creek in Williamsburg County is recorded on Cook's Map (1770) as Weatherspoons Ferry; some families still pronounce and/or spell it that way. On a hot dry day back in 1940 one of the York County Witherspoons evidenced the power of prayer. There'd been a long drought and the farms and flowers were hurting. At the meeting of the York Literary Club Miss Lettie Witherspoon was asked to give the invocation, which she concluded, "And, Lord, we need rain bad. Not just a little drizzle-drazzle, Lord. Send us a real gully-washer." Three and a half minutes after the Amen, the heavens opened up with a deluge.

Wofford
WAW-*fud*

This is one we had not included until we heard three different should-know-betters say WOOF-ud College. Affiliated with the South Carolina Conference of the United Methodist Church, Wofford College has operated continuously since its beginning in 1854. It is named for the Rev. Benjamin Wofford (1780–1850), a traveling Methodist minister and astute businessman. In his will he left $100,000 for endowing a college for men in his home district of Spartanburg—the largest gift for education in the South to that time. John Wesley Wofford (1841–1919), farmer, served in the state House and Senate from Spartanburg. Wofford Avenue in Forest Acres (east of Columbia) is one of ten streets named for South Carolina colleges in the Jackson Heights residential area.

Woodward
WOOD-uhd, WOOD-wuhd (OO as in foot)

Though the Aiken County family and some elsewhere in the state answer to WOOD-wuhd, the majority of the still-present family prefers the older pronunciation WOOD-uhd. Dr. Henry Woodward is known as the first English settler in South Carolina. In 1666 he traveled from North Carolina to Port Royal, where he lived with the Indians, learning their language and customs. Later he served as an interpreter for the English colonists. Woodward is also credited with being the first rice planter in America (around 1685), and South Carolina was the first colony to export rice. The story of the rice planters is told in *Seed from Madagascar* by Duncan Clinch Heyward, governor (1903–1907) and one of the last rice planters in the state. The town of Woodward (WOOD-wuhd; US 321) was established 25 miles north of Winnsboro on land given by Captain W. B. Woodward for the station and post office when the railroad came through. Woodward Street in Winnsboro is named for Thomas Woodward, prominent Colonial and Revolutionary citizen who was a Regulator in the Fairfield County area. The Regulators were a group of men who banded together to control outlaws and other undesirables in the backcountry, though it was complained that they soon began to abuse their power. Just before the Revolution Woodward emerged as the leader of the Whigs (or patriots) in the area. He was "a terror to evil-doers, and the dry bones of the Tories [Loyalists] shook at the very name of Woodward." Thomas William Woodward (1833–1902), Confederate major, planter, and state senator, owned Rock City, the granite quarries southwest of Winnsboro. As a junior he was expelled from South Carolina College in the "Steward's Hall" or "Great Biscuit Rebellion" in 1852, when over a hundred of the students demanded that the compulsory system of lodging and boarding at the college be abolished in favor of a voluntary boardinghouse arrangement. The trustees called their bluff and the students were obliged to fulfill their threat to leave.

Xuala

Shoo-AH-luh (oo as in boot)

Like Xulu, below, Xuala is a name that appears only in the very earliest Spanish accounts of the exploration of what is now the southeastern United States and in discussions by modern historians of those accounts. It is certain that De Soto crossed the Savannah in 1540 and traveled a section of what is now South Carolina before he turned west, but his precise route is the subject of wonderful disputes and wild conjectures among historians and archeologists. He appears to have followed very roughly the route of what is now US 1 up from Augusta into central South Carolina. At some point—but we would not *dare* suggest exactly *which* point—he turned west and reached the Cherokee settlement called Xuala (sometimes spelled with two Ls), which apparently was at the foot of the Appalachian Mountains and is generally thought to have been in what is now Oconee County, in the extreme northwest corner of South Carolina. *Hoo-AH-luh* and *Zoo-AH-luh* are defensible pronunciations, but Shoo-AH-luh is what most historians say, so it is the pronunciation we recommend.

Xulu

Hoo-Loo (oo as in hoop)

This word is used a couple of times in the narratives of the early Spanish explorers and may be merely a variant of Xuala. However, it is taken to mean the Cherokee Territory, which encompassed the southern Appalachians, extending nearly as far south as present-day Atlanta in Georgia and extended as far east as present-day Cheraw in South Carolina. For some reason historians, if they acknowledge the term at all, tend to pronounce it Hoo-Loo, although Shoo-Loo or Zoo-Loo may be closer to what the inhabitants of the region were actually saying to those first European explorers.

Yeamans
YAE-munz

Yeamans Hall is a plantation on Goose Creek (once known as Yeamans Creek) in Charleston County. The plantation was long in the family of Thomas Smith, son of the first Landgrave Smith. It was probably around 1800 that the name Yeamans Hall was given to the estate. Sir John Yeamans was governor of the colony settled on the west bank of the Ashley River from 1672 until his death in 1674.

Yemassee
YEM-uh-SEE

The Yemassee, also spelled Yamassee, were an Indian tribe who fought against the British colonists in the lowcountry of South Carolina in 1715 and 1716. The uprising is the subject of *The Yemassee*, the best-known novel of William Gilmore Simms, South Carolina's leading nineteenth-century man of letters. The word may mean old men or old women—those left at the village while the young braves went out to hunt or fight. The present town of Yemassee is in Hampton and Beaufort counties on US 17A at SC 68.

zip
ZIP

It's not the pronunciation; it's the meaning that may confuse. To the score-conscious sports fan, zip means zero. To the letter writer, zip code is the five numbers in the address placed after the town and state. But for Clemson College cadets of Depression days, zip was Sunday night supper's dessert: corn bread drowned in syrup—and it was SUH-rup then too.